RV CAMPING GUIDE FOR BEGINNERS

YOUR BLUEPRINT TO CONFIDENTLY SET UP YOUR RV AT ANY CAMPSITE, CONQUER MAINTENANCE CHALLENGES, AND STAY ON A BUDGET WHILE ON VACATION

RAIN TUCKER

© **Copyright Christine R Padula 2024 - All rights reserved.**

The content within this book may not be reproduced, duplicated or transmitted without direct written permission from the author or the publisher.

Under no circumstances will any blame or legal responsibility be held against the publisher, or author, for any damages, reparation, or monetary loss due to the information contained within this book. Either directly or indirectly. You are responsible for your own choices, actions, and results.

Legal Notice:

This book is copyright protected. This book is only for personal use. You cannot amend, distribute, sell, use, quote or paraphrase any part, of the content within this book, without the consent of the author or publisher.

Disclaimer Notice:

Please note the information contained within this document is for educational and entertainment purposes only. All effort has been expended to present accurate, up-to-date, and reliable, complete information. No warranties of any kind are declared or implied. Readers acknowledge that the author is not engaging in the rendering of legal, financial, medical or professional advice. The content within this book has been derived from various sources. Please consult a licensed professional before attempting any techniques outlined in this book.

By reading this document, the reader agrees that under no circumstances is the author responsible for any losses, direct or indirect, which are incurred as a result of the use of the information contained within this document, including, but not limited to, — errors, omissions, or inaccuracies.

CONTENTS

Introduction	v
1. WHAT SHOULD I KNOW ABOUT RV CAMPING?	1
An Overview of RVs	1
The Evolution of RVS	3
Dispelling Common Myths	5
Myth #1: I need a special license.	6
Myth #2: You cannot take short trips.	8
Myth #3: You can't take RVs to cities.	8
Myth #4: RVing is expensive.	10
Myth #5: RV maintenance is too much work.	11
Myth #6: RVs are only for old people.	12
Myth #7: You can't RV with pets.	12
Myth #8: You have to stay at an RV park.	13
Myth #9: RVs are stinky.	14
Myth #10: An RV starter kit has everything you will need.	15
What's Next?	16
2. WHICH RV IS RIGHT FOR ME?	17
Travel Trailers	19
Class A	21
Class B	22
Class C	24
Fifth Wheel	26
Pop-Up Campers	27
Toy Haulers	29
3. WHAT DO I NEED TO MAKE MY TRIPS SUCCESSFUL?	32
The 25 Tools You Should Have on Hand	34
Ask Yourself These Questions First	35
The 20 RV Kitchen Accessory Must Haves	41
How to Keep Items from Moving Around in Your RV Kitchen Cupboards	46
The 10 Foods to Store in Your RV	46
The 15 Essential Toiletries to Pack	49
The 10 Items of Clothing to Take on Every RV Trip	52
The 30 Essentials to Not Forget	53

4. WHAT DO I DO UPON ARRIVAL AND DEPARTURE?	61
Regular Maintenance Checks Before Any Trip	62
Arriving at the Campground	65
Setting Up Camp	67
Breaking Down Camp	73
5. WHAT ARE COMMON ISSUES I SHOULD BE AWARE OF AND AVOID?	79
Attaching Breakaway Cable to Receiver	80
Tire Blowouts	81
Leaky Roofs and Windows	82
Toilet Issues	83
Other Plumbing Issues	84
Battery Problems	85
6. HOW CAN I STAY ON BUDGET WHILE RV CAMPING?	88
Prepare Meals Ahead of Time	89
Join RV Clubs	90
Plan Free Outdoor Outings and Activities	91
Plan for Bad Weather	92
Try Boondocking	92
7. HOW DO I WINTERIZE OR STORE MY RV?	94
Winterizing Your RV	96
The Steps	97
Storing Your RV	101
Pulling Your RV Out of Storage	104
RVing in the Winter	106
8. IS FULL-TIME RV LIVING RIGHT FOR ME?	110
The RV Lifestyle	111
Helpful Tips and Tricks	112
RV Living With Kids	116
Conclusion	119
On the Road Together	121
Bibliography	123
About the Author	129

INTRODUCTION

 "I don't need therapy, I just need to go camping."

— UNKNOWN

Some of my earliest and fondest memories of camping are with my grandparents in their RV when I was a kid. We went camping at least one weekend a month, and during the summers, we would hop from one campground to the next.

It was magical. The aroma of roasting marshmallows, the cozy feeling of snuggling in my heated blanket, the refreshing feeling of the cool air on your face as soon as you stepped outside in the morning, and the savory smell of bacon filling the air.

Over the years, I went from an innocent bystander to a capable participant, helping my grandfather set up and break down camp and my grandmother map out our next adventure. I eventually learned how to help with almost every aspect of the camping journey.

After spending years alongside my grandparents, I understood all the inner workings of our trips and felt like camping wasn't just something we did - it was a proud part of my identity.

When I was in my late teens, I knew that I wanted to get an RV so my future kids could experience the same magic I had as a child. I started saving immediately and was able to purchase my first used RV when I was in my early 20s!

One of the unique aspects of RV camping is that it brings families and friends closer together than other types of vacations - literally! Since you are living in such close quarters and spending so much time together, it gives families a chance to reconnect with each other on a deeper level.

RVing prompts you to bond with the people around you and have those heartfelt conversations that you may not normally be open to if you were just on a regular vacation. It also gives your family more opportunities to spend quality time together by enjoying activities like playing card games or swimming in lakes or rivers at the campsite.

Plus, it's much more cost-effective than other types of vacations. You don't have to pay for plane tickets or hotel rooms since all of your accommodations are provided by your RV camper itself. Even those on tight budgets can still enjoy the great outdoors without breaking the bank.

And, perhaps, my number one favorite thing about the camping lifestyle is that it allows you to explore new places - all without being confined by conventional travel restrictions or schedules. You can take as long as you want at each location and never have to worry about making sure your flights arrive on time or not having access to a familiar bed —it's all taken care of with your RV camper!

Did I know everything there was to know about RV camping just from my childhood adventures alone? Definitely not. I thought I did, but through the years and lots of trial and error, I've finally been able to perfect my skills and come away with a comprehensive knowledge of successful RV camping, and I am here to pass it along to you.

One of the reasons why I love RVing so much is because you're constantly learning and exploring. Even with all my years of expertise, I still manage to learn a little something new on every camping trip. Each mishap or maintenance issue - and each nuance between the different campgrounds I visit - teaches me something helpful about RV camping.

Regardless of the learning curve, RV camping has changed my life in immeasurable ways, and it's sure to do the same for you. With that said, there are a few tips you'll want to keep in mind before you hit the open road.

If you've ever seen the movie RV, starring Robin Williams, you probably already know that it is possible to rent an RV for a week and take off on your next adventure. You don't technically have to have any working knowledge of the different types of RVs, how to find a campsite, how to deal with a tire blowout, or how to recharge an RV battery.

But, again, if you've ever watched that movie, you likely are aware that not only is it really not a good idea to go into this experience blind, without any background knowledge, but it can, at times, be downright dangerous. I'll never forget the scene where Robin's character forgets to chock the tires and the RV ends up rolling directly into a lake (ouch).

Like anything in life, RV camping does require a bit of preparation and know-how. I've been camping my entire life, and again, there's still always more for me to learn.

But I have mastered the basics - that is, I know everything there is to know in order to make a trip safe, enjoyable, and free of major catastrophes.

Fortunately, you're in the right place. While you could spend hours searching the internet for solutions to common RV camping problems, the reality is that the internet won't always be available to you.

For one, the internet is rife with misinformation and bad advice. It's hard to know where to look to find accurate information, and you'll likely spend days searching for answers to your simplest questions.

Not only that, but RV camping is filled with experiences that you can't possibly imagine happening to you until…well, until they happen to you!

For example, eighteen years ago, I went winter RVing for the first time in my own rig, and I completely didn't realize I would need to use a heated water hose or insulate my gray and black water supplies. It's an innocent enough mistake, but unfortunately, it caused all of my pipes and valves to freeze up, then expand and explode. It was a lesson I wished I could have learned without spending hundreds of dollars on repair bills.

I also can't tell you the number of times I've been out in the woods with no cell signal and been hours away from the closest town. Out there in the sticks, emergencies and mishaps still happen (and this is, in fact, where they are most likely to occur), but without cell service to Google search the problem, I've been out of luck.

That's where this book will come in handy. By having a copy of it by your side whenever you hit the open road, you'll be well-equipped to handle any challenge that comes your way.

In these pages, I've boiled down decades of RV camping experience to give you the roadmap to everything you'll need while on the road in your RV (no pun intended). You'll get all the shortcuts to successfully set up your RV at any campsite, prepare your RV to avoid any costly mistakes and budget appropriately to explore the great outdoors on your own terms.

After all, the whole point of going camping is to get away from the stressors of life - not to stress you out more.

So what do you think? Are you ready to become an RV camping expert? Let's dive in!

1

WHAT SHOULD I KNOW ABOUT RV CAMPING?

 "A crowded camper is better than an empty castle."

— UNKNOWN

Before we dive into the nitty gritty of caring for your RV, finding activities, maintaining your rig, and so on, it's important to first cover the basics.

After all, you wouldn't build a house without pouring the foundation first. Let's take a closer look at the bare bones of the topic - what are RVs, and what are some key facts you need to know?

An Overview of RVs

RVs, or recreational vehicles, are mobile homes that can be used for a variety of purposes, from weekend camping trips to extended cross-country road trips. While the term "RV" is often used interchangeably with "motorhome," there are actually several distinct types of RVs.

There are three main types of recreational vehicles—motorhomes, travel trailers, and fifth wheels. In general, a motorhome is a self-contained driving unit, or in other words, an RV that has an engine and a steering wheel built in. Travel trailers and fifth wheels are different in that they cannot be driven on their own, so you must have another vehicle that can tow them. These categories of recreational vehicles can be broken down even further.

Motorhomes come in styles ranging from Class A to Class C. The difference between them is based on the size and structure of the vehicle; Class A motorhomes are larger with more luxurious amenities, while Class C motorhomes offer a more compact design.

Travel trailers are one of the most common types of towable trailers. They come in a variety of sizes and shapes and can often sleep up to seven people.

Generally, travel trailers range from 16 feet long all the way up to 40 feet long and contain all the amenities you need on an outdoor adventure, such as a kitchen, bathroom, sleeping area, and storage space. They can also be outfitted with special features like air conditioning, slide-outs, and outdoor showers.

A toy hauler is essentially a hybrid between a travel trailer and a cargo trailer—it has both living space as well as additional storage space for toys such as ATVs or dirt bikes. Toy haulers come in many different sizes but typically have enough room for seating and beds, just like a regular travel trailer. The main difference is that they also have extra storage space in the back for items like off-road vehicles or motorcycles.

These are great for hauling small boats, too, like kayaks. I've found this feature to be especially handy when on the road.

Fifth-wheel or gooseneck trailers are larger than traditional travel trailers because they attach directly to your truck bed rather than being pulled behind it via a hitch ball connection.

This larger size makes them ideal for larger families who need more living space while still having access to plenty of storage options inside their trailers. Plus, fifth wheel/Gooseneck trailers typically provide enhanced stability while driving compared to traditional travel trailers due to their unique design.

If you're unsure which of these types of RVs is right for you or want to learn more about them, don't worry - we'll cover that in more detail below.

The Evolution of RVS

RV technology has come a long way since its inception. Whether you're an RV enthusiast or just curious about the history of RVs, this section will provide a timeline of their evolution. From the first hand-built motorhome in 1904 to the cutting-edge RVs of today, here's everything you need to know about the history and development of RVs.

It all starts back in the 1800s, back in our pioneering days.

In the 1800s, Romani communities traveled around Europe and North America in horse-drawn wagons known as "vardos." These wagons served as mobile homes and featured amenities like beds and cooking stoves. Although they weren't equipped with toilets or bathrooms, they provided shelter from the elements and enabled Romani people to enjoy some degree of mobility.

The first motorhome was built onto an automobile in 1904 by William Hawley Bowlus, who was inspired by his experience living in vardos with Romani people during his travels abroad.

His motorhome was constructed from a Model T Ford chassis he purchased from Henry Ford himself. The vehicle was equipped with a kitchenette, two beds, storage space for clothing and dishes, two kerosene lamps for lighting, and even a battery-powered phonograph for entertainment!

It may not sound like much now, but at the time, it was quite exquisite.

The 1920s saw the rise of campers and caravans—mobile homes that could be towed behind automobiles using ball hitches or drawbars. At this point, camping and life on the road, in general, had become increasingly popular. Americans were becoming more entranced with the idea of wilderness, and as the country's cities grew and we became more closely tied to urban areas, many Americans still had the desire to explore the wild portions of the world.

The RVs of the early 1920s were fully connected, with the house portion unable to be disconnected from the automobile. Motorhomes were restricted to car-friendly roads only and were extremely pricey.

But then, the travel trailer was invented.

These vehicles were much smaller than traditional motorhomes but still provided basic amenities like beds, kitchenettes, cabinets for storage space, and windows that allowed light into the vehicle while traveling.

The popularity of these travel trailers increased significantly during this decade due to their affordability compared to larger motorhomes. They were more functional, too, with tent canvases that broke down into a collapsible frame. It was easy to purchase a fully-equipped, manufactured tent trailer by the late 1920s.

By the 1930s, mobile homes evolved even further. Tent trailers had become the norm for people who couldn't afford the larger, clunkier, and more expensive mobile home, but they didn't offer quite as much protection.

Despite the fact that many manufacturers claimed their tent trailers were "fully waterproof," this was rarely the case. Campers found themselves (and their belongings) soaked by unexpected rainstorms, and manufacturers knew they had to find a way to solve this issue.

The RVs of the 1930s morphed into new camping trailers with hard sides. They were equipped with various amenities, including iceboxes, cupboards, built-in furniture, stoves, and more.

Though they weren't large - about six feet wide and nine feet long - they quickly rose to popularity. Known as "Covered Wagons," these machines became a favored alternative to the less-protective tent trailers of the 1920s.

With the second World War preoccupying most of America's attention during the 1940s, there wasn't much innovation in terms of RV technology until the 1950s. Returning soldiers were interested in inexpensive ways to travel and unwind, so the country's major RV manufacturers began adding new improvements to the existing models.

A few amenities that were added in the 1950s included plumbing, refrigeration, wall-to-wall carpeting, and multiple bathrooms. Multiple big-name manufacturers entered the scene in the 1950s, too, many of whom are still well-known today (like Airstream, Winnebago, and Ford).

Luxury was a top priority in the 1950s. People wanted to get away from home but not feel as though they were roughing it in the wilderness. Now, we call this "glamping" - but back then, they just called it "style." RVs were larger and more like stylish homes, with some unique RVs even containing portable swimming pools and built-in diving boards!

It was in the 1950s that the term "motorhome" became part of everyday lingo, and when the recreational vehicles we recognize today really began to take form.

Today, a typical 34-foot Class A motorhome has multiple bedrooms and televisions. There are full kitchens and, in some cases, multiple bathrooms. Low-maintenance travelers might be more interested in fifth-wheels and toy haulers, which look more like the original "Covered Wagon" of the 1930s.

Regardless of which model you choose or where you choose to travel, it's clear that recreational vehicles have come a long way since the 1800s.

Dispelling Common Myths

Even though RVing is close to my heart - and there's a large community of full-timers and weekend warriors who love it - you may have heard some not-so-positive rumors that have deterred you from trying RV camping at all yet.

Let's discuss them to set your mind at ease.

Myth #1: I need a special license.

One widespread myth about RVing is that you need a special license to drive your recreational vehicle. This is simply not true. In fact, any driver over the age of 18 with a valid driver's license can operate an RV —as long as it meets certain size and weight requirements. That being said, it's always important to check your state's specific laws on RVing in case there are any additional regulations or restrictions in place.

When it comes to the size and weight requirements for RVs, these vary by state as well.

Generally speaking, though, if your vehicle weighs under 26,001 pounds (11,794 kilograms), then it will qualify as a "light truck," meaning you won't need any additional licensing credentials beyond what you already have as a driver over 18 with a valid permit.

On the other hand, if your vehicle weighs more than 26,001 pounds (11,794 kilograms), then you will likely need a commercial driver's license (CDL).

It's important to look into the restrictions set forth by your own state's DMV and to pay close attention to any restrictions wherever you might be traveling. That's the best way to make sure you are road legal and that you have the training necessary to hit the road.

Of course, it never hurts to get some formal training. Even if you don't need to have a special license to drive your RV, learning how to safely operate and maneuver the vehicle is important.

RV driving courses provide you with all the tools and knowledge necessary to become familiar with the various features of RVs and how they work.

From understanding engine sizes and weights to knowing what kind of trailer hitch set-up works best for your rig, these courses provide invaluable information that can help you make more informed buying decisions.

Plus, taking an RV driving course gives you hands-on experience so that when it comes time to hit the open road, you feel confident in your ability to handle any situation that may arise.

Another benefit of taking an RV driving course is that it helps ensure your safety on the open road. Even after being so familiar with my grandpa driving the RV, it really took me by surprise to discover how different it was to be the one actually sitting in the driver's seat. My grandpa taught me a lot of the basics, but I still sought out additional training to help me learn everything I needed to know.

Knowledge is power. After all, it only takes one turn at the wrong angle to ruin your RV trip!

An RV isn't a small little car by any means. It's a large machine with the potential to go quite fast. If you're nervous or not sure what you're doing, you could hurt yourself or others. That's why familiarizing yourself with the rules of the road and the logistics of operating such a large machine is so important.

Not only that, but as an RV driver, it is your responsibility to other drivers on the road to learn everything you can about how to operate an RV so you can keep everyone safe.

Some examples?

For starters, understanding how to properly maneuver around tight corners or drive through high winds can be crucial when traveling in an RV. These courses also cover topics such as proper loading techniques and how to use emergency equipment should something go wrong while on your journey.

When signing up for an RV driving course, you will get access to experienced professionals who can provide insight into all aspects of operating and maintaining your vehicle. From advice on choosing a good campsite or navigating tricky terrain, these instructors are there as guides throughout your entire learning process—and beyond!

So while it's a myth that you always need a special license to drive an RV, know that, license or no license, taking a training course in how to drive one never hurts. Remember: Knowledge is power!

Myth #2: You cannot take short trips.

When most people think about taking a trip in an RV, they often envision a lengthy journey across multiple states or even countries. But there are plenty of benefits to taking shorter trips instead.

With a short RV adventure, you get to experience all the joys of RV life without having to commit to days or weeks away from home. You also get to save money on fuel costs since you won't be driving as far, and you'll usually have fewer expenses when it comes to food and lodging since you won't be gone for as long.

Plus, with shorter trips, there's less pressure to cram everything into one journey; if you run out of time during one adventure, there's always another opportunity waiting around the corner!

Personally, shorter trips are my favorite. You don't have to think quite as much about what to bring with you or what routes to go. If you have limited time off work, this is also an ideal way to get your camping fix.

RVs are perfect for a quick weekend getaway; whether it's to the Adirondacks for some hiking, to Cape Cod to hit the beach, or simply enjoying some quality family time at your favorite nearby campground, even weekend getaways can become unforgettable adventures on four wheels.

Myth #3: You can't take RVs to cities.

Are you an RV enthusiast who's been told that you can't take your vehicle into a city? Fear not! Despite what many people believe, it is possible to explore cities and urban areas by RV.

In fact, exploring cities in my RV is one of my favorite things to do. There are lots of benefits - you don't have to worry about not having cell reception or being far from a hospital in case of an emergency, and there are plenty of restaurants, bars, and other attractions to check out, too.

Contrary to popular belief, RVs are not limited to open highways and vast stretches of roadway. With proper planning, you can take your RV into city centers and explore the sights and sounds in comfort. I won't say that driving an RV down crowded city streets is the easiest thing I've ever done - but with practice, you'll find that it becomes surprisingly manageable.

That said, there are a few considerations to keep in mind when taking your RV into a city. It's important to research local laws regarding camping within city limits; some cities may have laws restricting overnight parking or camping on public land within their borders.

If you're visiting from out-of-state, make sure to check if there are any restrictions on out-of-state vehicles entering the area. You may want to research roads with low traffic density and look up nearby parking lots where RVs are allowed so that you can avoid narrow streets or busy highways where your vehicle might be too large for safe maneuvering.

Make sure your route takes into account any potential one-way streets or traffic restrictions due to construction work or other circumstances so that getting stuck isn't an issue during your adventure.

Taking your RV into a city allows you to enjoy all of its attractions without having to worry about finding accommodation or getting around town quickly enough. You'll have everything you need right at hand—from food preparation facilities to sleeping quarters—making your stay even more convenient and enjoyable than ever before.

That said, some cities will be easier to maneuver in than others. If you're new to RV camping, I wouldn't make your first urban excursion in a city like Manhattan or Boston, both of which have heavy traffic and extremely difficult-to-navigate streets.

Better cities to consider as a first-time RV driver might include:

- Las Vegas, Nevada
- Washington, D.C.
- Phoenix, Arizona
- Denver, Colorado

Not only do these cities tend to offer the best opportunities for sightseeing, but they're also fairly easy to navigate in a large vehicle like an RV.

Myth #4: RVing is expensive.

One common myth about RVing is that it's more expensive than other forms of travel. While it's true that RVs come with some upfront costs, such as purchasing or leasing an RV, fuel, insurance, maintenance, and storage fees, these costs can be minimized through careful planning.

For example, if you plan on taking long RV trips often, you can purchase a Class A or Class C motorhome. These types of RVs typically cost less per mile compared to renting an RV from a dealer or company when taking into account all expenses like insurance and fuel.

Also, most states offer discounts on campground fees to seniors and veterans, which can significantly reduce your overall costs.

Another way to save money on your road trip is by using discount programs offered by some hotels and campgrounds. These programs often offer discounts for memberships which can help you save up to 50% off nightly stays in certain areas.

Furthermore, many cities across the country have free public parks where you can park your RV overnight without having to pay camping fees! This is great for travelers who are looking to save money while still enjoying their road trip adventures in their own vehicle instead of sleeping in a hotel room each night. Free public parks tend to be most common in the Midwest, in my experience.

Other areas, like Salt Lake City, allow RVs to park for free overnight on the side of the road on certain streets (for up to 48 hours).

Finally, if you want to reduce your overall expenses while traveling in your RV, consider joining one of the many campground clubs available online.

These clubs provide special deals on campsites throughout the country. They also offer access to exclusive discounts on entertainment activities like golf courses or amusement parks that would otherwise be too costly for non-membership holders. Some examples include Escapees RV Club, Boondockers Welcome, and Passport America.

Plus, these clubs usually provide members with useful tips for finding cheaper camping spots during peak season so you can get even more out of your vacation budget.

Myth #5: RV maintenance is too much work.

For those who have never been RVing, the thought of taking care of a recreational vehicle may seem daunting. As with any vehicle, regular maintenance is important to keep it in top condition. One common myth about RVing is that RV maintenance is too much work, and while there *is* maintenance, it's not as challenging as you might think.

In fact, with a few simple tips and tricks, you can keep your RV running like new for years to come.

Of course, you should always take the time to familiarize yourself with your vehicle. Read through your owner's manual and get to know the different components of your RV. You should also learn how to check tire pressure and other basic checks so that you can do them on a regular basis. Make sure you know where all the filters are located so you can easily replace them when needed.

It's a good idea to take your RV in for a check-up every year or two. Even if it appears to be running smoothly, an experienced technician will be able to spot small issues before they become big problems down the line.

A professional can also inspect the electrical system and give you advice on how to keep it running at peak performance levels. Most importantly, they'll be able to tell you what preventative measures need to be taken in order for your RV to stay in tip-top shape over time.

Remember, maintenance is the key to keeping your RV in good shape for years to come, but that doesn't mean you have to go it alone. I'll do my best to give you as many helpful maintenance tips as I can to help you get started. However, if you don't feel comfortable or just don't have the time to tackle all of your maintenance yourself, there's no shame in hiring someone to help you.

I've done this for the last few seasons of winterizing my RV, and honestly, it's a lifesaver. The amount of time I save is worth the small amount of money it costs - plus, there's the peace of mind in knowing it has been done correctly before the bad winter weather sets in and begins wreaking havoc on my machine.

Myth #6: RVs are only for old people.

If you are considering getting an RV, you may have heard that they are only for people of a certain age. This misconception couldn't be further from the truth! RVing is popular among all ages and can be a great way to bond with family, friends, and even strangers.

The most common reason this misconception is perpetuated is because of how RVs are portrayed in media and advertising. Movies, TV shows, and commercials depicting older people in RVs oftentimes use stereotypes or outdated ideas about RVers.

This type of media often portrays an unrealistic idea of what it means to own an RV or go on an RV trip. As a result, people who don't fit into the stereotype can feel like they don't belong in the community.

In reality, there are many different types of people who enjoy RVing: young families looking for adventure, single professionals searching for their next office escape, retirees exploring the country…the list goes on! No matter your age or background, there's a place for you in the world of RVing.

Myth #7: You can't RV with pets.

If you've ever considered taking your pet on a long-distance road trip, RV camping is an ideal way to do it. Unfortunately, there's a common misconception that you can't RV camp with pets – but fortunately, that isn't the case.

Before setting off on your journey, it's important to make sure that your campground of choice is pet-friendly. Not all campgrounds are, so be sure to check ahead of time. If you plan on staying in multiple places during your trip, be sure to double-check that all destinations are also pet-friendly before booking.

You should also consider whether or not the grounds will provide enough space for your pet to roam around safely - and whether there are any nearby attractions that allow pets. Once you have everything squared away, then it's time to get ready for the trip!

Once you arrive at your destination, there will no doubt be lots of fun activities awaiting both you and your four-legged companion! Whether it's hiking trails or beaches nearby, having fun outdoors is one of the best features of camping with pets - but please make sure Fido stays leashed at all times for safety reasons.

You can definitely RV with pets, especially if you take the time to make sure your pet is well-cared for while you're on the road. It's yet another advantage that RV camping has over traditional forms of travel. If you've ever had to pay for a pet-friendly hotel room, you know how tough these are to find - and how costly they are to book.

Myth #8: You have to stay at an RV park.

If you're a new RVer, you may have heard of the common misconception that you must stay at an RV park every time you hit the road. It's true that some RVers like to stick to campgrounds, but there are lots of other options for those willing to explore a little more.

Boondocking is one great alternative to campgrounds or RV parks, especially if you are looking to truly immerse yourself in nature. Boondocking means camping in a remote area with no hookups or amenities. There are lots of free boondocking spots all over the country, and some are even on public land, so you don't have to worry about getting permission from a private landowner.

Of course, if your rig is equipped with solar or other off-grid power sources, fresh water storage tanks, and gray water tanks, then boondocking can be even easier and more convenient.

Dry camping is similar to boondocking in that no hookups are available. However, this type of camping spot is usually closer to established areas like parking lots and rest areas where free or cheap resources are available nearby. Dry camping sites may also be found at established campgrounds and serve as a cheaper alternative to the full hookup sites.

Many state parks offer dry camping sites along with full hookup campsites, so it's worth checking out each option before deciding which one would suit your needs best.

If you're looking for something unique and unexpected, Harvest Hosts might be just what you need! This membership program allows members access to hundreds of farms and wineries across the United States, where they can park overnight at no cost (in exchange for supporting these businesses by purchasing their products). You get the peace and quiet of camping in nature while also having access to interesting places that most people never get to experience firsthand!

Myth #9: RVs are stinky.

When it comes to RV camping, one of the biggest myths is that RVs are smelly, dingy, and just plain gross. After all, who wants to spend their vacation inside a stinky vehicle? The truth is that an RV doesn't have to be smelly or dirty at all.

When it comes to keeping your RV smelling fresh and free of odors, ventilation is key. The more air circulation you have in your RV, the less chance there is for airborne particles or moisture to get trapped and cause unpleasant smells. Make sure you open up any windows or vents when you're not using the space—especially if you've been cooking or have had a lot of people over—to allow fresh air in and stale air out.

The best way to ensure your RV won't smell bad is by keeping it clean. Vacuum often (at least once a week) to keep pet hair, dust, dirt, and allergens from collecting on surfaces. Wipe down counters with a disinfectant after meals and mop floors with a mild cleaner every few days.

If you're camping near water, don't forget to rinse out your shower after each use because soap residue can lead to unpleasant smells as well as mold growth!

When people ask me whether I think my RV is stinky, I'm honest with them - no, it's not. At least, it's no dirtier or stinkier than my own house. The key is that you have to treat your RV like any other living space. You're not going to leave old food lying around, and you're not going to let your dog jump up on the counters.

Basic hygiene and upkeep are the keys to keeping things fresh.

As long as you're vigilant about cleaning and ventilation - just as you would be within your own house - you shouldn't have any problems with unwanted odors inside your rig. Just because it's a mobile home doesn't mean it needs to be a messy home!

Myth #10: An RV starter kit has everything you will need.

So, you're thinking about getting an RV, but you've heard a rumor that there exists a magical starter kit for all your needs. But is it true? Can one simple purchase get you everything you need to get out on the open road in your new home away from home?

These kits get a lot of attention, marketed as "all-in-one" and "totally inclusive." While they can be helpful in some regards, the truth is that you're going to need to do some extra legwork to make sure you actually have everything you need.

There is no single RV starter kit that contains every single item you will ever need for your adventure. While some kits can be helpful in providing basics like cookware, utensils, towels, bedding, and cleaning supplies, they are far from comprehensive and often don't contain the items that are most important for a successful RV trip.

For instance, many kits don't include any of the items you'll need to maintain your rig while on the road. That means no tools or spare parts (like fuses, lightbulbs, or hoses) necessary for keeping your RV running smoothly - not to mention any of the camping equipment needed once you reach your destination. Additionally, most kits won't have items like toilet paper or other toiletries - which are essential when setting up camp in remote areas and/or places without access to stores.

Finally, some kits might even come with outdated or subpar supplies that won't last long enough to make them worth purchasing. In other words, if you're looking for quality products at an affordable price point that can stand up to regular use over years of travel, it's best to purchase these items separately instead of relying on what comes with an RV starter kit.

What's Next?

Now you know a brief history of RV camping - and some of the most common modern myths we hold about RV camping today.

RV camping has been around since people were traveling by covered wagon - but let's face it, it's much more enjoyable now! Our modern amenities, from flushing toilets to televisions and, yes, a luxury RV with a built-in swimming pool and diving board, are features that our ancestors would have thought to be pure fantasy!

But before you can enjoy all that RV camping has to offer, you need to figure out which RV is right for you. It's definitely not a one-size-fits-all solution, but it's important to take the time to make sure you've found the perfect match.

In the next chapter, we'll take a closer look at how to find your dream RV.

2

WHICH RV IS RIGHT FOR ME?

 "It always rains on tents. Rainstorms will travel thousands of miles, against prevailing winds for the opportunity to rain on a tent."

— DAVE BARRY

Don't get me wrong - I like tent camping. But there's something to be said about the protection that a good RV offers from the elements!

In that regard, just about any old RV will do. However, if you want to really enjoy your trips, you need to find the RV that's right for you.

When I bought my first RV, I honestly thought it would be with me for life. It was perfect - and despite being a little on the smaller side, it worked well for what I wanted to do with it.

Of course, that changed.

With two children, my family had outgrown our small RV for our vacation trips.

We could no longer fit comfortably in the cramped quarters, not to mention there wasn't even enough storage space for all of our camping gear.

After a long drive to go camping one weekend, my partner and I faced the height of our inevitable growing pain. Just imagine the joy of kids screaming and fighting with each other in the background of a small RV while trying to maneuver the narrow lanes on the highway.

I'm being sarcastic, of course - but in all seriousness, that's when we knew it was time to upgrade to a bigger RV.

When my partner and I went shopping for a bigger RV, we got more than just an upgraded vehicle - we found one with bunk beds, plenty of storage space, and roomy seating. We figured this would be perfect for our family trips and getting our kids to stop arguing.

Little did we know the great impact it would lead to - our kids suddenly became *excited* about going camping, coming up with creative ways to decorate their bunk beds, and begging us for more camping trips! Not only did we get an upgrade in size, but we also ended up getting an upgrade in fun!

One of the best ways to make sure you're setting yourself up for success is to make sure you have the right gear. That starts with the ideal camper. While there's nothing wrong with starting with a smaller RV (and one that you can afford), you may find that you end up upgrading later on.

In a perfect world, we would all have a million dollars to spend on an RV that parks itself, cleans itself, and maintains itself - but we don't live in a perfect world (and I also don't think that exists yet - Elon Musk, help us out, will ya?).

So in the absence of such a beautiful feat of engineering, we have to make do with what we have. That starts with selecting the best RV we can afford.

Before you get started in your search, I recommend making a priority list (a "wish list," if you will) of everything you want in your RV. At the top of this list should be what you plan to tow it with (or if you want an RV that is a self-contained unit and not meant to be towed). You'll be limited in your selections if you drive a small car or don't have a car at all, but don't worry - there are still options.

Once you've got that figured out, think about things like how much space you want inside, what your budget looks like, and how many people you'll be traveling with. You'll also want to consider whether you'll be toting anything else along on your trips (like boats or ATVs).

With that in mind, let's take a closer look at the most popular types of RVs that exist so you can figure out which category might be the best place for you to start your search!

Travel Trailers

Travel trailers are recreational vehicles (RVs) that can be towed by a truck, van, SUV, or even a car. They come in many different shapes, sizes, and styles; some look like mini-homes, while others are smaller and more compact. Essentially, a travel trailer could be equated to a tent on wheels. It has no self-steering or driving capabilities and is instead meant to be towed.

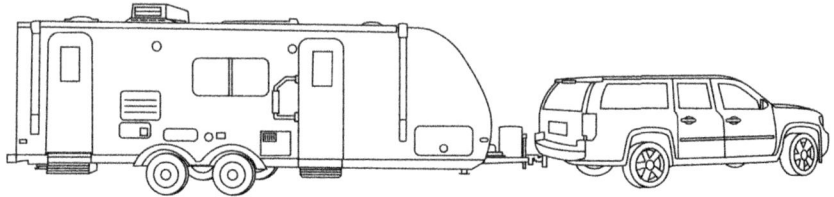

Example sketch of a travel trailer (left) connected to a tow vehicle (right).

They offer amenities such as beds, bathrooms, kitchens, entertainment areas, and storage space–allowing campers to enjoy their vacation without leaving the comfort of their home away from home.

The best thing about travel trailers is their cost–they are typically much cheaper than larger RVs such as motorhomes or fifth wheels. They tend to be more economical since they don't require large vehicles to tow them. Travel trailers also tend to be easier to maintain than motorhomes since most of the maintenance can be done yourself without having to visit a mechanic.

Moreover, insurance costs for travel trailers are generally lower than those for larger RVs since they have fewer components that need coverage. Finally, due to their smaller size and portability, you have more flexibility when it comes to arranging your travel plans–there's no need for large trucks or vans!

One drawback of travel trailers is that if you want your experience on the road to be truly luxurious, it could still cost you quite a bit of money–especially if you go for one with all the bells and whistles. The average travel trailer will cost between $11,000 and $50,000, depending on the features and size you've chosen, but some can be as much as $200,000! As you can see, there's a ton of variation here.

Also, bear in mind that not all vehicles are suitable for hauling a travel trailer–it takes certain types of engines with high torque capacity in order for your car or truck to tow it safely over long distances at highway speeds. While travel trailers are generally the best option for people with smaller vehicles, that doesn't mean every travel trailer will work for every small vehicle - pay attention to the specs!

Then there's the comfort aspect. This is a big one for me. Unlike motorhomes, which allow travelers to stay inside while on the move, travel trailers require users to stop the vehicle and step outside (into potentially inclement weather conditions) each time they need something from inside (like food).

Finally, although some people may find them comfortable enough for extended periods of time on the road, most travelers will find them less luxurious than larger RVs when it comes to amenities like beds or showers. This means that depending on how much space you need and how often you plan on traveling in your trailer –you may want something bigger instead!

Here are a few quick tips for choosing the right travel trailer:

- **Decide on the best size:** Choosing a travel trailer that is the right size is essential. You'll need to consider not only aesthetics and comfort but also whether or not your pickup truck or car can pull it. Make sure there's enough space inside for all the gear you want to take with you on your travels.

- **Make a wish list:** Make a list of all the features you'd like in your travel trailer, and then determine which are "must-haves" and "non-negotiables." This will help ensure that you don't end up with a trailer that doesn't meet your expectations.
- **Is there enough storage?:** Storage is important in any RV, especially if you plan on living in it full-time or using it often throughout the year. Make sure to check out how much storage space there is so that you can keep your trailer organized and keep the clutter packed away.

Class A

Class A motorhomes are the largest type of recreational vehicle. They range from 24-45 feet long and feature slide-outs for additional living space. These vehicles have a truck-style chassis (picture a coach bus from the outside) with either a gas or diesel engine and come with all of the amenities you would expect from a home on wheels—bathroom, kitchen, sleeping quarters, and entertainment systems.

Example sketch of a Class A motorhome.

Class A motorhomes offer plenty of storage space as well as comfort and convenience while traveling on the road. They are ideal if you plan on spending extended periods of time in your vehicle or if you need extra space for family members or pets. However, they do require more fuel than some other types of RVs and can be more difficult to maneuver due to their size.

Most models come with slide-outs (that expand the living area), air conditioning and heating systems, bathrooms with showers and toilets, and kitchenettes or full kitchens with microwaves, stoves, and refrigerators. They are designed to provide an easy way to travel without having to stay in hotels or motels.

One of the greatest benefits of owning a Class A RV is that you can bring all your home comforts along with you when you travel. This includes everything from your bedding to your favorite food items!

Not only that, but they give you room to stretch out while on the road and provide more privacy than hotels or other types of accommodations do. For that reason, they can save money in the long run when compared to paying for lodging during extended trips.

That said, when compared to travel trailers, Class As require more maintenance due to their larger size and additional components like generators or water systems. Of course, they're also self-contained units that have actual engines in them, too. They can be expensive upfront; even used models tend to cost thousands of dollars depending on their condition. Fuel costs can add up quickly due to the weight of these motorhomes as well.

Class A RVs are often referred to as "luxury motorhomes" because they are the largest and most luxurious option available. They are also some of the most expensive on the market because of their size and amenities, with the average Class A RV coming in at around $250,000.

But if you want maximum comfort and convenience during your travels, then a Class A RV may be worth the extra cost.

Class B

A Class B RV—sometimes referred to as a campervan or conversion van—is a recreational vehicle built with an existing van chassis. They typically have all the amenities of a standard motorhome, like sleeping space, dining area, bathroom facilities, kitchenette, and storage space; however, they are usually much smaller in size than traditional motorhomes or travel trailers.

Class B RVs are also often less expensive than other types of RVs due to their size and ease of maneuverability.

Example sketch of a Class B motorhome.

These vehicles usually range from 16-25 feet long and typically include kitchenettes, bathrooms, sleeping accommodations, and entertainment systems. Again, they are built on a van chassis, which makes them easier to drive than Class A models but also means there is less storage space available.

The most obvious pro to owning a Class B RV is its small size which allows for easy maneuverability in tight spaces. Plus, because it's built on top of an existing van chassis, there isn't much additional work required during the manufacturing process, so Class B RVs tend to be less expensive than other types of RVs. They're a good option for someone who doesn't have a vehicle suitable for hitching up a travel trailer as well.

On the downside, however, due to their small size, these vehicles can often feel cramped if you plan on taking extended trips with multiple passengers or family members. Also, since they don't have any separate living areas, they may not offer enough privacy if that's something you're looking for in an RV experience.

For a Class B RV, expect to pay $60,000 for a basic model or as high as $240,000 for the most premium high-end model.

If you're thinking about buying your own Class B RV, there are a few things that you should consider beforehand.

Ensure the vehicle is properly inspected by a certified mechanic (even if it's being sold "as-is"), and research various makes & models online before committing to anything. That way, you know exactly what kind of features each one offers and how much money you should expect to spend overall.

It pays to shop around at different dealerships or private sellers before making your decision so that you get the best possible deal on your dream ride!

Class C

A Class C RV is an intermediate-sized vehicle that provides more space than a van but is smaller and easier to drive than a bus-style motorhome.

Class C motorhomes are similar to Class B models in terms of size, but they are built on a truck chassis instead of a van chassis. This means that they offer more storage space than Class B models but still provide all of the amenities needed for comfortable travel, such as bathrooms, kitchens, sleeping quarters, and entertainment systems.

One of the primary advantages of a Class C RV over other types of RVs is its size. These vehicles are typically between 21 and 35 feet in length and can sleep up to 8 people depending on the model.

This size makes them an ideal choice for families or groups who want extra room without having to maneuver excessively large vehicles around. Since they are smaller than traditional motorhomes, they tend to use less fuel and cost less money to operate.

Another benefit of Class C RVs is their affordability compared to other types of motorhomes. They often provide many of the same amenities as larger models at a much lower price point—so you can get all the comforts of home without breaking the bank! Some even come with slide-outs so you can expand your living space when parked in campgrounds or other spots where you have plenty of room.

Example sketch of a Class C motorhome.

Not only that, but they can come with cab-over sections, which provide additional living space without sacrificing maneuverability or fuel economy, as some larger RVs do. A cab-over section is just as it sounds; it's that portion of the RV that extends over the cabin of the driver and passenger seats, and many times a bed is conveniently placed there.

The biggest drawback associated with Class C RVs is their interior design; they tend to be divided into two sections which can limit some activities, such as entertaining guests or playing games while on the road.

These vehicles don't offer quite as much storage space as their larger counterparts due to their compact designs—so if you plan on taking long trips with lots of luggage, this might not be the best option for you.

The average cost for a new Class C RV ranges from $50,000 - $100,000 depending on make/model/amenities/size/etc., though there are some models available for less than $50K if you're looking for something basic and budget-friendly.

With the increasing popularity of RV travel, it can take time to decide which type of recreational vehicle is right for you. Class A, B, and C RVs all have their own unique benefits and drawbacks; understanding these distinctions, as highlighted above, will help you make an informed decision about which type of RV is best suited to your lifestyle and needs.

Once you've narrowed down your choices based on research and budget constraints, it's time to take each potential model out for a test drive.

This isn't just an opportunity to get familiar with all the features offered by different models—it also gives you a chance to see how comfortable the vehicle feels while driving and how easy it is to maneuver in tight spaces or over bumpy terrain if necessary.

Be sure to take notes during each test drive so that you can compare them side-by-side once all test drives have been completed.

Fifth Wheel

A fifth-wheel RV, or "fifth-wheel trailer" as it is sometimes called, is a type of recreational vehicle designed for long-distance travel due to its stable structure that creates a smooth ride. It consists of an enclosed living space built within an elongated trailer that has two axles and four wheels.

Example sketch of a fifth wheel trailer (left) connected to a tow vehicle (right).

It is typically towed by a large pickup truck and hitched over the rear axle at the back of the truck. The raised bed area of the fifth wheel fits over the back of a pickup truck for additional stability and to make it incredibly easy to "tow." This hitch for the RV has a round wheel-like shape and is what gives the fifth wheel its name! Along with offering more stability while driving than other types of recreational vehicles, it tends to have more interior space as well due to its raised bed area.

The biggest advantage of fifth-wheel RVs is their size. Because they are much larger than traditional trailers, they offer more space for you to spread out and relax while on the road. Plus, these large rigs typically have additional sleeping areas that can be used for guests or family members.

On top of that, fifth wheels generally have more storage compartments than other types of RVs, making it easier to pack all your essentials without having to sacrifice valuable living space.

On the downside, fifth wheels tend to be more expensive than other types of campers due largely in part to their size and amenities. That being said, if you're looking for a long-term investment or plan on spending extended periods on the road with family or friends, then this type of RV may be worth considering despite its higher cost.

Also, because these rigs are so large, they require a special truck or vehicle with a high tow capacity in order to pull them safely. Make sure to factor this into your decision as well.

The cost of fifth-wheel RVs varies depending on make and model, but the average price for a new one is between $20-$60K, with some luxury models costing upwards of $100K+. If you're looking for something used, then you should expect prices to start around $12K (depending on age and condition).

Pop-Up Campers

If you're looking for an RV camping experience that won't break the bank and is easy to tow, then you should consider buying a pop-up camper. These campers offer an affordable alternative to traditional RVs and a comfortable way to get out in nature.

A pop-up camper is a type of recreational vehicle that can be pulled by most cars and SUVs. It has collapsible sides that "pop up" when set up, turning it into a small travel trailer with sleeping accommodations. Pop-up campers are typically small enough that they can fit in most driveways or garages when not in use, making them ideal for those who need to store their RV when not traveling.

Example sketch of a pop-up camper.

One of the main advantages of owning a pop-up camper is that they are much lighter than other types of RVs, making them easier to tow behind your vehicle.

They also tend to be less expensive than other types of campers, which makes them great for those who are just getting into camping or those on a budget. Plus, since they open up like a tent, set-up time is usually much faster than with other RVs.

As with our other options, there are some downsides to owning a pop-up camper as well. For one thing, these campers don't have nearly as many amenities as larger RVs do. This means that if you need running water or electricity while camping, then this isn't going to be the best option for you.

As was the case with our "Covered Wagon" we talked about from the early 1900s, these campers can be more prone to leaks due to their canvas walls and roofs. They don't come with air conditioning units installed, so if you need cooling during the hot summer months, then you'll have to purchase one separately and install it yourself.

The cost of pop-up campers varies widely depending on make and model but generally ranges from about $4k-$15k when purchased new from dealerships.

Used models can often be found for much cheaper on sites like Craigslist or eBay, but it's important to do your research before purchasing one secondhand since these campers may not have been maintained properly by previous owners and may require repairs/maintenance before being used again safely.

Pop-up campers are great for those who want an RV-like experience without spending too much money or having too heavy of an item towed behind their vehicle; however, they aren't quite as luxurious as other types of RVs, such as fifth wheels or travel trailers. These typically have more space and amenities included inside them (such as bathrooms).

Therefore, if luxury is what you seek, then perhaps another type of camper would better suit your needs!

Toy Haulers

Whether you're an off-roading enthusiast or a weekend warrior, toy haulers are a great way to get out and explore the world around you. With room for your toys, extra storage, and all the comforts of home, it's no wonder why toy hauler RVs have become so popular in recent years. But what exactly is a toy hauler RV?

A toy hauler RV is a type of recreational vehicle that comes equipped with an interior storage area known as a "garage." This garage can be used to store ATVs, dirt bikes, kayaks, fishing gear—basically, any kind of outdoor gear you need for your adventure. Many models also come with special features such as built-in generators, air conditioning units, slide-out rooms, and more.

The biggest benefit of owning a toy hauler RV is the ability to take your favorite "toys" on vacation with you.

No more worrying about trying to find space for your gear—it's all right there in your RV! You also won't have to worry about leaving expensive equipment behind when you leave home—you can just lock it up inside the garage!

On the downside, toy haulers tend to be heavier than regular travel trailers due to their extra weight from cargo capacity. This means they require more fuel and may not be suitable for smaller vehicles like cars or SUVs.

Example sketch of a toy hauler.

Toy haulers range in price from around $20,000 for an entry-level model all the way up to $100,000 for top-of-the-line luxury models. As far as used models go, prices vary widely depending on age and condition but generally start at around $10,000.

Toy haulers come in all shapes and sizes, from small pop-up models to large fifth-wheel trailers. Before you begin shopping, think about how much space you will need and what type of vehicle you plan on using to tow it. This will help narrow down your search and save time in the long run.

Choosing the Right RV

Before you begin shopping for an RV, it's important to consider your budget. You'll want to determine what type of RV fits within your budget and how much you are willing to spend.

Keep in mind that buying an RV isn't just about the purchase price; there will also be ongoing maintenance costs and potential upgrades that may need to be made over time. All of these expenses should be factored into your budget before making a final decision.

The size of the RV is another important factor to consider when shopping. Your ideal RV size will depend on how many people will be using it and how much space they will need while traveling together.

If you plan on taking long trips with multiple people, then a larger option might suit your needs better than a smaller one. But if only two or three of you are traveling together, then a smaller option may be more appropriate as it will save on fuel costs and storage space when not in use.

Last but not least, comfort is an important factor when selecting an RV. After all, no one wants to stay in cramped quarters during their vacation! Consider what amenities are most important to you, such as air conditioning, bathrooms and showers, kitchens, entertainment centers, and sleeping areas, before deciding which type of RV is best for your family's needs.

Choosing the right type of RV for your needs can seem like a daunting task, but with careful consideration of budget, size, and comfort level, it doesn't have to be. The type of RV you select will depend on many variables, including whether or not you want to tow it, what kind of vehicle you have and its towing capabilities, and how many people you plan on traveling with.

Hopefully, this last section has been helpful to you in acquainting you with the many different types of RVs that exist. That said, knowledge is power - so take the time to visit your local RV dealership and try some out for size. Nothing compares to seeing the actual RVs (and, ideally, test-driving them!) to get a feel for what might be right for you.

No matter what kind of RV you end up with, you're going to have great experiences while out there on the road and mingling with nature. Next, we'll go over how to make your trips successful (and enjoyable).

Buying the RV is just the first step. You still have the whole open road to explore!

3

WHAT DO I NEED TO MAKE MY TRIPS SUCCESSFUL?

 "RV camping: where you can walk among strangers with a bag of dog poop in your hand and still strike up a conversation."

— UNKNOWN

I'll never forget our family's famous RV trip in 2016.

It's a trip that will forever live in infamy - or at least, one that probably scarred most of the members of my family (and perhaps a few random strangers, too).

Here's what happened (and don't worry - the intro quote will make sense in just a few minutes).

On a trip across the country, we decided to veer a little off the beaten path and check out some of the area's more remote hiking trails. We knew we would be able to park the RV relatively close to the trailhead we wanted to check out, so we weren't worried about finding a campsite.

We had everything we needed in the RV, and since we didn't have to make any campground reservations or worry about any of those sorts of logistics, our plan was to park, hike in, take in the sights, hike back out, and stay in the RV overnight.

What we did not plan for was the fact that both of my children would neglect to bring their water bottles on the hike (you'll understand, if you have kids of a certain age, that there comes a time that forms a gray area in which you expect them to be capable of doing certain things, and most times they are…except when they aren't!).

No big deal - it was only a ten-mile hike. We'd hiked much further than that in the past, and since it was a relatively cool day and a flat trail, we figured they could just drink out of their parents' water bottles until we made it back to the RV.

What we didn't plan for was the fact that my partner's water bottle had a slow leak and was empty (and his vest soaked) by the time we reached the turn-around spot. With only one water bottle to spare, I gave the rest of my water to my kids, and my partner and I resorted to drinking water out of a (clear and safe-looking) brook near the trail.

Big. Mistake.

If you have any experience with hiking, you are probably already laughing your butt off at our idiocy! But even from all my RV camping experience as a child, I didn't have a ton of backwoods experience, and I figured, since it was running water (not stagnant) and clear-looking, we would be safe.

I can't say for sure whether it was the water, the stress of the day, or something else that got to us, but by the time we got to the RV, my partner and I were arguing vehemently about who would get to use the toilet first (I won).

Or so I thought.

When I reached for the toilet paper after I had finished my…experience…I discovered that there was only one single solitary square left. Frantic, I rummaged through the bin in the bathroom, only to realize that we had never replenished our TP supply at our last stop to restock our supplies.

My partner relegated himself to coffee filters, and by the time we made it to the next stop, we were absolutely desperate.

We pulled into the next campground desperate, not sure where the next convenience store was, but fortunately, another camper took pity on us and gave us some of their extra TP.

Since that experience, I've realized that people are naturally kind and generous - but they are much kinder if it's your dog's poop you're worried about and not your own!

The moral of the story is this - preparation is key.

Pack the extra toilet paper. Pack the extra water bottles. Pack the water purification tablets. Heck, pack the extra coffee filters. You never know what you're going to need or when.

It's far better to be prepared than to be the person carrying a plastic bag of clothes you'll never be able to wear again around a campsite.

Just trust me.

The 25 Tools You Should Have on Hand

All poop jokes aside, it's important to be prepared when you head out on the open road.

One of the most serious aspects of preparedness is on the mechanical side. Unfortunately, no matter how well you maintain and care for your RV, stuff happens. That's why it's a good idea to have a basic set of tools with you to deal with these emergencies.

Where to Store Your RV Tools

RVs are a great way to explore the outdoors and go on adventures, but having the right tools on hand is essential for keeping your RV in top condition. Keeping them organized is critical for quick access in an emergency, as well as regular maintenance.

The first step in organizing your RV tools is to keep them out of sight and out of the way. Consider putting lightweight items like screwdrivers, pliers, and hammers beneath the seats or tables (contained in a toolbox) in your RV. This is a great place to store items that you don't want cluttering up your countertops or taking up space in drawers.

Your drawers and cabinets are ideal places to store heavier tools such as wrenches or ratchets. You can also use drawer dividers or drawstring bags to organize smaller items such as screws, bolts, nuts, and washers, so they don't get lost. Make sure you label each bag or divider so you know exactly what it contains! This will make it much easier when it comes time for repairs and maintenance.

Tools like hammers, wrenches, pliers, screwdrivers, ratchets, and more can be stored on hooks along the walls of your RV. If you have a bit more room available, consider installing a pegboard so you can hang all of your tools up in one spot for easy access when needed (just make sure you choose one specifically for use in RVs so you don't have to worry about materials and tools flying around - if you can't find one, another good option is to find one meant for use in a contractor van. Same idea!).

This is especially helpful if you need several different wrenches for different jobs around the RV's engine compartment!

With that said, let's dive into what tools you might need on your RV adventures.

Ask Yourself These Questions First

Whether you've just bought your first RV or you're a veteran of the road, certain tools can make your journey smoother. But with so many options out there today, it can be difficult to know what to bring with you and what to leave behind. To help you decide, ask yourself these questions before packing up for your next trip.

How Handy Are You?

I, personally, am not the most mechanically inclined. I'm fortunate that my partner has a good mechanical wit about him, but even before we started RV camping together, I always made it a point to stock my RV with all the tools I could ever possibly need (even tools I wasn't totally sure how to use).

The reason? You never know what's going to happen. I'd rather have all the tools I need with me in case I break down - that way if I'm with somebody (or somebody stops to help me) with good mechanical knowledge, they have the tools necessary to help get me back on the road or at least to the closest repair shop.

How Much Space Do You Have?

This is probably the most important question to consider when selecting the tools for your RV trip. The size of your vehicle will determine how much space you have available for storage and will ultimately limit the size of the items you can bring.

If space is scarce, opt for smaller items like screwdrivers, hammers, and wrenches since these are typically some of the most useful tools when working on RVs.

How Far Will You Be Going?

The distance of your trip will also inform which tools you should bring along. For shorter trips, basic hand tools may be sufficient, but if you're going cross-country, then it's wise to invest in heavier-duty equipment like a drill.

Also, if you plan on traveling through remote areas, then it's best to bring along spare parts, such as extra hoses and fuses, in case something breaks down unexpectedly.

How Old is Your RV?

If your RV is older than 5 years old, then it's especially important to bring an array of diagnostic tools with you on your journey. Older vehicles may require more attention and maintenance than newer ones, so having a multimeter or voltage tester handy can save you time and money should any unexpected issues arise during your travels.

With these considerations in mind, these are the 25 tools I recommend to have on hand:

1. Air Compressor

This device allows you to quickly inflate or deflate your tires as needed, which can be helpful if you encounter rough terrain or need to adjust tire pressure for better fuel efficiency.

It's also great for inflating other items such as rafts and kayaks, beach balls, and even air mattresses for extra sleeping space.

2. Fix a Flat Kit

A flat kit is useful in case of a tire puncture or blowout during your camping trip. It comes with everything you need to repair the tire quickly and easily so that you can get back on the road without too much hassle. This kit should include items like a tire patch kit, valve stem core remover, tire plugger, and tube sealer—all of which will help get your tires back up and running in no time.

3. Tire Pressure Gauge

A tire pressure gauge is another important tool that you should have when camping with your RV. It's important to maintain proper tire pressure while traveling—this ensures fuel efficiency and reduces the risk of a blowout due to overinflation or underinflation. With this handy tool, checking tire pressure is quick and easy so that you can keep your ride safe at all times.

4. Cordless Drill and Drill Bit Set

If any repairs need to be made on the RV during your trip, having a cordless drill handy can really come in handy! A drill bit set should also be included so that you have all of the necessary bits needed for any job (screw-driving bits, hole saws, etc.). A drill can save you a ton of time when compared to using screwdrivers to check or replace RV components. Not only can it be used for larger maintenance tasks, but you can also use it to install hooks or other accessories within the RV.

5. Breaker Bar

A breaker bar is a long metal rod with a handle at one end and a socket wrench at the other end. It provides extra leverage so you can loosen stubborn nuts or bolts without putting too much strain on your hands or arms. It's always wise to have one of these in case any repairs need to be done while you're out camping, and they take up very little room in an RV's storage compartment.

6. Headlamp/Flashlight

No matter how well-lit the campsite is, it can be difficult to find things in the dark corners of an RV at night—so make sure you bring along a headlamp or flashlight! Not only will this help light up dark areas inside your RV, but it will also come in handy if you need to go outside after dark — like if there's an animal making noise near your campsite late at night!

7. Folding Hand Saw

A folding hand saw is ideal for cutting wood for a campfire, trimming branches away from your campsite, and any other small projects that may come up during your trip. It also takes up very little space in your RV storage area.

8. Shovel

You never know what kind of terrain you will encounter at each campsite, so having a shovel with you is always a smart idea. A shovel can help smooth out rocky areas so that it is more comfortable to walk on and make sure your tent stakes are securely in the ground. Plus, they're also perfect for burying campfire ashes or digging a sand pit by the beach if that's where you decide to set up camp!

9. Pliers

Pliers are another essential tool that can be used for many different tasks while RV camping. Pliers are great for repairing broken items around the campsite, tightening bolts on your RV's exterior components such as doors or windows, and helping remove difficult knots from cords and ropes used in setting up tents or tarps.

10. Utility Knife

If there's one tool everyone should bring along while camping, it's a utility knife! Having one handy will make life much easier if you need to cut rope, open packaging, carve wood, trim tree branches away from your campsite, or sharpen sticks for marshmallow roasting – the possibilities are endless! Just make sure to keep this tool safely stored away when not in use to prevent any accidents.

11. Hex Set

If anything needs fixing while you're out enjoying nature, having a hex set around will come in handy! These sets contain multiple sizes of hex keys which can be used to tighten screws or other fasteners on items around the campground, such as picnic tables or outdoor furniture.

12. Socket Set

A socket set is another must-have item when RV camping because these tools allow you to loosen and tighten nuts and bolts quickly and easily. Socket sets come in various sizes, so find one that fits all of the nuts and bolts on your vehicle before hitting the road!

13. Eternabond

Eternabond is a special type of tape used for sealing up holes and cracks in your RV, as well as providing a waterproof seal for windows and other surfaces. This tape can help keep moisture out of your RV and prevent small leaks from becoming bigger problems. It's easy to use, highly durable, and will last for years.

14. Caulk Gun

Whether you need to seal up a crack in your RV or just want to make sure the windows are airtight, having a caulk gun on hand is essential. This tool makes it easy to apply sealant quickly and evenly, ensuring that everything is properly sealed up before you hit the road.

15. Zip Ties

Zip ties are an incredibly versatile tool that can be used for numerous purposes while camping in your RV. You can use them to secure items inside your trailer, fasten down tarps, or even hang lights outside the vehicle. They're lightweight, affordable, and easily stored away when not in use.

16. Gorilla Tape

Gorilla Tape is an incredibly strong adhesive tape that is perfect for outdoor use due to its durability and waterproof properties. It's great for patching up holes or covering exposed wires in your vehicle — just make sure you remove any debris before applying it!

17. Ratchet Straps/Bungee Cords

Ratchet straps and bungee cords are invaluable when packing up an RV for camping trips. They allow you to securely tie down items inside the trailer so they don't shift around during transit — which can save you time (and headaches) when setting up camp later on!

18. Tow Strap and Chains

A tow strap and chains are essential items to bring on any RV trip. If something happens while you're on the road—like a flat tire or engine trouble—you can use these to tow your vehicle back to safety. Make sure you get good quality straps and chains that can handle the weight of your vehicle and can easily be hooked up to another car or truck if needed.

19. Multimeter

A multimeter is a tool that measures voltage, current, and resistance in electrical circuits. It's an essential part of troubleshooting in case of any electrical problem with your RV. With a multimeter, you can quickly identify issues like loose wires or incorrect wiring so that you can fix them before they become bigger problems down the road.

20. Electrical Tape

Whether it's fixing loose wires or patching up broken insulation, electrical tape will come in handy when it comes time to repair your RV. Electrical tape is also useful for labeling cords and wires so you can easily identify which one goes where when it's time to disconnect them.

21. Wire Cutters

Wire cutters are indispensable when it comes to cutting through thick wiring or clipping off portions of the wiring that cannot be used anymore. Wire cutters can even help cut through other materials like plastic and metal if needed.

22. Adjustable Wrench

An adjustable wrench is another must-have tool for your next camping trip, as it can help tighten and loosen nuts and bolts in hard-to-reach areas of your RV. Adjustable wrenches also come in handy when working with plumbing fixtures such as faucets, showers, and toilets that require tightening or loosening of nuts or screws in order to function properly.

23. Dremel Tool

If you need to make precise cuts or drill into difficult spots while camping, then bringing a Dremel tool is an absolute necessity! This small rotary power tool allows you to easily get into tight spaces without having to worry about damaging anything else around it. The Dremel tool also comes with various attachments so that you can use it for sanding, polishing, buffing, engraving, and much more!

24. Heat Gun

Heat guns are incredibly helpful when working with any plastic material found inside an RV, such as pipes or vents. Heat guns allow campers to shrink-wrap materials together quickly and efficiently without worrying about melting the plastic material itself. Heat guns also come in handy if you ever find yourself needing to bend PVC pipes or remove stubborn adhesive from surfaces.

25. Hammer

Lastly, no matter how many fancy power tools you have brought along with you on your journey - nothing beats having a hammer close by! A hammer comes in handy whenever something needs pounding down into place (such as tent stakes) or taken apart (such as broken furniture). Hammers are also great for smashing rocks apart, so they can be used as makeshift fire pits!

The 20 RV Kitchen Accessory Must Haves

While my partner is the go-to guy when it comes to RV repairs, I'm the master chef. I love whipping up breakfast, lunch, dinner, and snacks for my family, and when we hit the road in our RV, my cooking experiments don't stop.

A lot of people have the assumption that because RVs are small, there's not really enough room to cook in them. That couldn't be farther from the truth. I enjoy cooking in my RV, and while I've been known to kick the kids outside from time to time, the small size of my RV kitchen honestly makes life a little easier.

Why? There's no need to overcomplicate things. I don't have to worry about finding "x, y, z" new crockpot recipes. (Spoiler: It's because I barely have room for a crockpot.) I have just enough room for what I need or really want and nothing more or less.

Also - fewer dishes to wash. Bonus!

With that said, here are some of my RV kitchen must-haves. Choose to bring items from this list that feel essential or useful to you, and skip those that seem unnecessary.

1. Silverware

A great place to start stocking your RV kitchen is with some quality silverware. What kind of silverware should you get? I recommend finding a set that's lightweight and durable enough to handle meal prepping while on the road. Stainless steel flatware with wooden handles is both stylish and reliable, perfect for any RV traveler.

2. Kitchen Utensils

In addition to silverware, it's important to stock up on essential kitchen utensils like spatulas, ladles, serving spoons, tongs, and more. As with your silverware set, opt for utensils made of stainless steel or plastic that can withstand high temperatures without melting or warping.

3. Over-the-Sink Cutting Board

An over-the-sink cutting board is an absolute must for any RV kitchen! This type of cutting board fits snugly over your sink, so there's no need for extra counter space. Plus, this makes cleaning up afterward a breeze since all those scraps will go directly down into the sink!

4. Dish Rack

Even though space may be limited in an RV kitchen, it doesn't mean that you have to skip out on drying dishes after hand washing them. Investing in a foldable dish rack that can fit inside cabinets or drawers is a great way to save space while still getting the job done. You can also use it as extra countertop space when needed!

5. Toaster

For some people, having freshly baked toast in the morning is essential! To make sure you don't miss out on this luxury while traveling with an RV, invest in a compact two-slice toaster. This will take up minimal countertop space yet still provide plenty of toast each morning!

6. Coffee Maker

Few things compare to having freshly brewed coffee each morning—but where do you keep it when there's no room? A small single-cup coffee maker takes up minimal countertop space but still brews delicious coffee quickly and easily every time!

7. Cast Iron Skillet

A cast iron skillet is a great piece of equipment for any RV kitchen because it can handle a variety of tasks. From frying eggs and bacon to baking cornbread and cookies, a cast iron skillet can do it all. Plus, cast iron skillets are incredibly durable, so you don't have to worry about them breaking or warping on your journey.

8. Cookie Sheets

Cookie sheets are essential for anyone who likes to bake while they travel. They're ideal for making cookies, brownies, or other treats that require an even heat distribution over a large surface area. Plus, they're easy to clean and store flat when not in use!

9. Portable Propane Grill

A portable propane grill is perfect for anyone who wants to enjoy a delicious grilled meal while on the road. Portable grills come in all shapes and sizes, so you can choose one that fits perfectly into your RV kitchen set-up. Plus, since they run on propane gas, you don't have to worry about running out of fuel mid-cooking session!

10. Stackable Pots and Pans

Having stackable pots and pans makes cooking in an RV much easier because they take up less storage space than traditional pots and pans do.

11. Stackable Mixing Bowls

Mixing bowls are essential for anyone who likes to bake or prepare meals ahead of time when traveling in their RV. Stackable mixing bowls make it easy to store all your ingredients before cooking – plus, they save space compared with traditional mixing bowls since they can be stacked together when not in use.

12. Nutribullet

For those who want to make on-the-go smoothies, shakes, and even baby food while RVing, a Nutribullet is an invaluable tool. This compact blender comes with its own travel cup and lid, so you can make drinks or food wherever you go. Plus, it's small enough to store easily in your RV kitchen.

13. Water Filter

If you're camping in the wilderness, chances are there won't be access to clean drinking water. A portable water filter will ensure that your drinking water is safe and free of contaminants. It will also save you money by eliminating the need to buy bottled water at campsites or gas stations.

14. Knife Sets

A must-have for any kitchen–and especially an RV one–is a knife set that includes all the essentials like chef's knives, paring knives, steak knives, and more. Investing in quality knives will help you prepare meals quickly and efficiently while out on the road.

15. Collapsible Strainer

If space is limited in your RV kitchen, collapsible strainers can be a great addition to your set-up. These strainers fold up flat, so they take up minimal space while still allowing you to wash veggies or drain cooked pasta without taking up much real estate in your cupboards or counters.

16. RV Trash Can (Pop Up)

An RV trash can with a pop-up lid is essential for keeping your kitchen clean and organized while out on the road. These cans come in various sizes, so you can pick one that fits perfectly into your rig's interior design scheme without sacrificing storage space or convenience.

17. Collapsible Food Storage Containers

These containers are a must-have when it comes to organizing your kitchen in a compact space. They collapse down flat so that they take up less room than traditional plastic containers, making them great for limited spaces like an RV. Bonus - these containers come in a variety of sizes, so you can easily store different types of foods.

18. Collapsible Measuring Sets

Collapsible measuring sets come with spoons and cups that fold together neatly into one package, so they won't take up much space in your kitchen.

19. Instant Pot

Yes—an Instant Pot is only slightly smaller than a crockpot (depending on the size you get), but it has way more functionality. An Instant Pot is one of the most versatile tools in any kitchen – but especially one inside an RV! This multi-use appliance can do everything from pressure cooking to slow cooking and more. If you are going to opt for something that takes up a bit more space, I'd recommend a pressure cooker over a slow cooker so you can get more meal options from your equipment.

20. Roasting Sticks

Roasting sticks are perfect for any campfire cookout while on the road! They're lightweight and collapsible, so they don't take up a lot of room - plus, they make it easy to roast hot dogs, marshmallows (or anything else) over an open fire! In my opinion, this is probably the most important piece of equipment to have in your RV kitchen - how can you enjoy a campfire without s'mores, after all?

How to Keep Items from Moving Around in Your RV Kitchen Cupboards

If you're like most RVers, chances are you have experienced the frustration of trying to keep items organized in your RV kitchen cupboards. From spices and condiments to utensils and plates, it can be a challenge to keep everything from rolling around and sliding out of place as you drive down the road. Fortunately, with a little organization and the right products, it is possible to create a secure environment for all your kitchen items.

Lazy Susans and turntables are an excellent solution for organizing small items in your RV kitchen cupboards. These circular-shaped shelves allow you to spin them around so that all of your items are visible and easily accessible.

The best part? You don't have to worry about losing anything because everything will stay exactly where you left it! Plus, these devices are relatively inexpensive and easy to install.

Drawer dividers or sliding trays can be a great way to organize larger items in your RV kitchen cabinets, such as pots, pans, dishware, etc. These products come in various sizes, so you can find something that fits perfectly into whatever type of cabinet space you have available.

They also provide an easy way for you to quickly access the item that you need without having to dig through piles of other gear first. This makes cooking on the go much easier!

Non-slip mats are another great option for keeping all of your kitchen items from sliding around while driving down the road. Simply line each shelf with non-slip material such as felt or rubber mats before placing any dishes or other breakable items on them—and voila! Now, all of those pesky plates won't go flying out when you turn a corner!

The 10 Foods to Store in Your RV

This next section is very subjective. The food you store in your RV will depend largely on your family's preferences, dietary habits, and how much space you have available.

With that said, whenever we do any grocery shopping for our RV, there are a few questions we ask ourselves.

One is, how much room do we currently have? If our RV kitchen is already pretty packed, we don't want to overload it by buying a ton more food that's just going to go bad.

We also try to veer toward food that has a longer shelf life. I'm talking about things like canned vegetables, dry beans, grains, etc. We don't usually buy a lot of processed food - but we also don't buy a ton of fresh fruits and vegetables while we're on the road. We buy what we know we will eat within the next few days, and a little backup. Here are some of our staples.

1. Canned Beans and Vegetables

When stocking up for your next cross-country journey, don't forget to include canned beans and vegetables. Not only are these items easy to store, but they provide essential protein and vitamins as well. From lentils and chickpeas to corn and carrots, there are countless options for adding healthy ingredients to your meals without having to break out the grill or stovetop.

2. Olive Oil

Using a little olive oil can go a long way toward making an otherwise bland meal come alive with flavor. It also provides good fats that can help keep you feeling energized throughout the day—an important factor when you're driving around in an RV all day long! Olive oil is shelf stable and can be easily stored in any size pantry, making it perfect for those who want great taste without taking up too much space.

3. Boxed or Canned Soup

Sometimes, you just don't have time (or energy) to cook a full meal from scratch—that's where boxed or canned soups come in handy! Soups are easy to prepare (just heat them up!), plus they come in many different flavors, so there's something for everyone's tastes. Plus, when made correctly, soups can provide ample amounts of protein and other nutrients that will keep you going throughout the day.

4. Pasta and Sauce

When it comes to convenience food staples, pasta is king! Not only does pasta offer complex carbohydrates for sustained energy levels throughout the day, but it also pairs perfectly with a variety of sauces for endless flavor combinations. And since pasta stores well in almost any size pantry or cupboard, it makes perfect sense to stock up before setting out on your next adventure!

5. Powdered Milk

Powdered milk is another great option when it comes to storing food in an RV pantry because not only is powdered milk shelf stable, but it also provides numerous health benefits, such as calcium and vitamin D, which help build strong bones and teeth.

Plus, powdered milk takes up much less space than traditional cow's milk, so if storage space is limited, then this might be a better option for you! Don't forget you might want milk for your coffee, too, so be sure to buy enough to get you through.

6. Canned Tuna

Canned tuna is a great way to get some protein in your diet without having to cook up a big meal. It's also incredibly versatile and can be used in salads, sandwiches, and even pasta. Since it's shelf-stable, it doesn't need to be refrigerated until it's opened.

7. Rice

Rice is one of those pantry staples that never goes bad. It's an excellent source of energy and carbohydrates, making it a great choice for any meal plan. Plus, it has a long shelf life—perfect for RVs! In addition to being versatile and nutritious, rice comes in many different forms, so you'll never get bored with your meals.

8. Coffee and Tea

Whether you prefer coffee or tea (or both!), keeping some on hand will ensure that everyone has something warm to start their day with. Coffee beans tend to stay fresher longer than pre-ground varieties, so if you have room for a grinder, they are worth considering, too.

9. Spices and Herbs

Adding spices and herbs can take even the simplest recipes from boring to amazing! Having these items on hand allows you to customize any dish with whatever flavor profile you desire.

10. Trail Mix, Nuts, and Dried Fruit

Trail mix isn't just for hikers anymore! It makes an excellent snack or topping on yogurt or oatmeal for breakfast. Nuts are also high in protein and can be used as toppings or as part of snacking mixes. Dried fruit is another great snack option that will add sweetness without needing any refrigeration—perfect when space is limited!

The 15 Essential Toiletries to Pack

Again, this next section is also somewhat subjective, but it's a good place to start when it comes to essential toiletries.

You may find that there are certain items you would rather include or omit from the list. For example, I wear contact lenses, so it's important for me to pack extra contacts and cleaning solutions.

I don't take prescription medications, but if you're on any kind of meds, be sure to add those to your packing list - in fact, those should be at the very top of your list since they'll be the hardest to get your hands on if you run out while you're on the road (items like toothpaste, on the other hand, are pretty easy to secure).

1. Soap

Soap is a no-brainer when it comes to packing for any trip. It's important to keep your skin clean and healthy while on the road. Make sure you pack enough soap for everyone!

2. Shampoo and Conditioner

Like soap, shampoo and conditioner should also be included in your toiletry bag. Don't forget to bring along a travel-size bottle of each so that you don't have to lug around large bottles in your RV.

3. Dry Shampoo

Dry shampoo is great for those days when you don't have time for a full shower. It can help revive limp hair and keep it looking fresh until you can find a time or place to wash it properly.

4. Body Wipes (or Baby Wipes)

Body wipes are perfect for those days when you just need something quick and easy. They can help freshen up your body without having to take a full shower or bath. Baby wipes are inexpensive alternatives you may want to consider.

5. Razor

If you want to look put together while on the road, then make sure not to forget the razor! Whether it's an electric shaver or a disposable one, having one handy will ensure that you look presentable at all times.

6. Toothbrush and Toothpaste

Of course, this one is a no-brainer! But don't forget to include travel-sized toothpaste tubes in your bag; they're small enough to fit in any nook or cranny in your RV storage space.

7. Lotion

The dry air inside an RV can do a number on your skin. Make sure to pack some lotion to keep yourself hydrated throughout your travels.

8. Deodorant

This is another must-have item, especially if you plan on taking part in any physical activities during your trip. You don't want to be the person everyone is avoiding because of body odor! Look for natural deodorants with ingredients like baking soda and essential oils — they tend to be more gentle on sensitive skin than traditional antiperspirants.

9. Sunscreen and Aloe Vera

Sun protection is essential while traveling in an RV — after all, you'll likely be spending long days out in the sun exploring different areas of the country! Pack plenty of sunscreen with broad spectrum SPF 30 or higher (water-resistant varieties are ideal).

If you forget sunscreen or end up getting too much sun one day, aloe vera gel can come in handy as well since it helps reduce inflammation and discomfort from sunburns.

10. Feminine Hygiene Products

You never know when supplies will run low or if these items will be available at your destination. Having some on hand can come in handy should an emergency arise.

11. Tweezers

Tweezers can help with any unwanted splinters or ticks that may find their way into your skin while camping outdoors.

12. Insect Repellent

Mosquitoes and other bugs are common when spending time outside—it's important to bring insect repellent along with you on your trip in order to keep yourself protected from bites.

13. Prescriptions

It goes without saying that any prescriptions needed should be brought along when going on a camping trip. Make sure to pack enough medication for the entire duration of your stay as well as some extra "just in case" pills—just in case anything unexpected happens during the trip.

14. Basic First Aid Kit

Having a basic first aid kit is an absolute must-have item whenever going camping—you never know when an accident may happen while out exploring nature! You also never know how far away the nearest hospital or medical attendant might be. Include bandages, antiseptic ointment, gauze pads, antibiotics ointment, burn cream, aspirin/ibuprofen, antihistamines (for allergies), safety pins, and tweezers.

15. Hair Brush

It goes without saying that keeping hair brushed regularly will help maintain good hygiene and prevent frustrating knots while out camping. Plus, it's always nice to look put together, even if you're roughing it outside!

The 10 Items of Clothing to Take on Every RV Trip

Again - highly subjective, but this list is a good place to start.

1. Socks

You'll want to bring several pairs of socks with you so that your feet stay warm and dry throughout your trip. Make sure to choose socks made from breathable materials like cotton or wool so that they won't cause your feet to sweat too much.

2. Underwear

A good rule of thumb is to bring at least two pairs of underwear for every day of your RV trip. If you plan on taking a few days off the grid, then it's a good idea to bring more than enough in case something happens and you need a backup pair.

3. Long Sleeve Shirts and Jackets

Layering is key when it comes to surviving the cold nights spent in an RV. Make sure to pack at least one long-sleeved shirt and one jacket for each person traveling with you in order to keep everyone warm and cozy during your time away from home.

4. Pants

Whether it's jeans, chinos, or hiking pants, make sure to pack at least two pairs of pants per person on your trip so that everyone has plenty of options when it comes time to get dressed each day (and night).

5. Shorts

The weather can change quickly when out on the open road, so it's best to be prepared with some shorts just in case the temperatures outside start rising unexpectedly!

6. Swimwear

If your RV has its own pool or if there are public pools nearby, make sure everyone packs their swimsuits before embarking on the journey!

7. Rain Gear

You never know when Mother Nature might have something else planned for your vacation, which is why it's important to always have rain gear handy just in case! Pack umbrellas, rain ponchos, rubber boots—whatever it takes for each member of the family to stay dry during bad weather days!

8. Hats

Keeping your head covered is essential - especially during those hot summer months.

9. Extra Shoes

One of the best features of RVing is that it gives you the opportunity to explore your surroundings—whether that means hiking through a national park or simply strolling around a quaint small town. No matter what your plans are, you'll want to make sure you have a good pair of comfortable walking shoes so you can fully enjoy your adventure.

10. Loungewear

While you may like to dress up for some of your RVing pass-bys or destinations, remember to pack some comfortable lounge clothes like sweatpants, relaxed T-shirts, tank tops, or whatever makes you comfortable while relaxing in or around your RV!

The 30 Essentials to Not Forget

Last but not least…the rest of the "stuff."

As you gain more experience as an RV camper, you'll find that there are other items you want to bring with you on the road. You may not think of these on your first, second, or even third trip - and again, whether or not you truly feel you need them will vary depending on your personal preferences.

With that said, though, here are some of the other items I always like to pack.

1. Water Pressure Regulator

This is one of the most important pieces of equipment to bring on an RV trip. It helps regulate the water pressure as it enters your RV's plumbing system, preventing damage and potential leaks. The regulator should be installed at the entrance point of your RV's connection to the external water supply.

2. Potable Water Drinking Hose

You'll also need to bring along a potable water drinking hose so you can easily connect from the outside water source to your drinking faucet inside. This will allow you to connect to a potable water source that's available at some (though not all) campsites.

Be sure to check that this hose is specifically certified safe for drinking water before you set off on your journey!

3. RV Sewer Kit

Of course, you'll also want to pack an RV sewer kit so you can properly dispose of waste while you're out on the road. This kit typically includes a hose and attachments for connecting with other campsites or dump stations where waste can be disposed of safely and legally.

4. Extra Blankets

If temperatures drop during your stay, having extra blankets is essential! Pack a few extra blankets and pillows just in case you need them during those chilly nights in the woods.

5. Camping Chairs

These are great for sitting around campfires or simply providing additional seating when needed. Invest in lightweight camping chairs that fold down easily so they don't take up too much space in the RV.

6. Camping Lantern

A camping lantern is essential for any RV trip. Not only do they provide light in the dark night, but they also help set the mood for a cozy evening spent with friends or family. A good camping lantern should be lightweight, durable, and waterproof—so it won't get ruined if it rains while you're out on your trip.

7. Disinfecting Wipes

Keeping your hands clean is important not just during an RV trip but all year round. That's why it's important to bring along disinfecting wipes wherever you go in your RV. These wipes are great for cleaning up messes and wiping down surfaces before eating or handling food and drinks. Plus, they're small enough to fit easily in any bag or storage compartment.

8. Fire Extinguisher

No matter where you're headed on your RV trip, a fire extinguisher is an absolute must-have item for safety purposes. It's always better to be prepared than sorry!

Make sure your fire extinguisher is rated properly based on the size of your vehicle so that it will work correctly in case of an emergency situation. Don't forget to check its expiration date before every trip as well.

9. Electrical Adapters

You never know when electrical adapters might come in handy while on an RV trip! Whether you need to plug something into a wall outlet or charge multiple devices at once from one outlet, having the right adapters can save you time and hassle when trying to power up electronics like phones, laptops, cameras, and more. Look for adapters that work with several types of outlets so that you can use them anywhere without having to carry around multiple adapters for different countries or regions.

10. National Park Guidebook

If you plan on visiting national parks as part of your RV trip, then it's essential that you bring along a guidebook outlining all the rules and regulations associated with each park—including details like speed limits and noise levels allowed within each park's boundaries.

11. Portable Power Station

A portable power station is essential for anyone taking an RV trip. It's especially helpful if you plan on camping in remote areas or will be away from hookups for extended periods of time. You can use it to charge phones, tablets, laptops, cameras, and other electronics without having access to an outlet.

12. Fuse Kit

A fuse kit is another item that every RVer should have on hand. If something goes wrong with the electrical system in your RV, you'll need a fuse kit to replace any blown fuses and get everything working again. Make sure you get one that includes spare fuses as well as a multimeter for testing circuits.

13. Bluetooth Radio

Bringing along a Bluetooth radio is also a great idea when taking an RV trip. Not only does it provide entertainment while you're on the road, but it also allows you to easily connect with friends back home via phone calls or video chat.

14. Portable Surge Protector

If there's one thing that can ruin any outdoor adventure quickly, it's getting hit by lightning or experiencing a power surge – both of which can damage all sorts of electronic devices and appliances inside your RV. A portable surge protector is just the thing for keeping these potential disasters at bay by redirecting excess electricity away from sensitive equipment like TVs and laptops.

15. RV GPS

An RV GPS is essential if you plan on doing any off-the-beaten-path exploration while traveling in your motorhome or trailer. Not only will it help keep track of where you are going and where you have been, but it also helps avoid narrow roads or low bridges that may be challenging for larger vehicles – saving time, money, and possible headaches down the line.

16. Travel Laundry Bag

A travel laundry bag is perfect for keeping your dirty clothes separate from your clean ones while on the road. It's lightweight and can easily be hung up or tucked away in a corner when not in use. Plus, it helps keep your RV smelling fresh!

17. Folding Table

A folding table is great for dining outside or setting up games like cards and checkers. They come in all shapes and sizes, so you're sure to find one that fits perfectly in your RV. Plus, they are very easy to set up and take down when not in use.

18. Grill and Grilling Utensils

Whether you're cooking hotdogs over an open flame or grilling up some burgers, having or using a grill is essential for any outdoor adventure. Be sure to pack all of the necessary grilling utensils - tongs, spatulas, etc. - so that you can cook with ease if you get the opportunity to use a grill at your campsite.

19. HotSpot Antenna

If you want to stay connected while on the open road, then a hot spot antenna is a must-have accessory for your RV travels. It allows you to access wireless internet almost anywhere there's cell phone service. So, no matter where you go, you'll always have reliable internet access!

20. We Boost

If cell phone service isn't available at your destination or if it's weak where you are staying, then WeBoost is definitely something that should be added to your packing list. This device boosts signal strength so that you can make calls and send texts without worrying about dropped connections or slow speeds.

21. Leveling Blocks and Chocks

Having level ground is important when it comes to setting up your camper. Leveling blocks and chocks will help you ensure that your RV is positioned correctly so you can enjoy a comfortable stay while camping. They will also help prevent any damage from occurring due to uneven ground or instability. Make sure to bring several sets, as they come in handy more often than you might think!

22. Generator

A generator can be incredibly useful if you want to power electronic devices or use appliances while camping without hookups. Generators are available in different sizes depending on what type of activities you plan on doing while camping. If you plan on using the generator frequently, consider investing in one with an electric start for ease of use.

23. Paper Products

It's easy to forget paper products when packing for a long journey in your RV, but they can be essential during your trip. Paper products such as paper towels, plates, and silverware are all necessary items that will make life easier on the road. You don't have to bring too many; just enough for the duration of your stay!

24. Tarps

A tarp or two can come in handy if it rains during your adventure or if you need some extra protection from the sun's harsh rays. Tarps are lightweight and easy to transport, so make sure to pack them along with some rain gear like jackets or ponchos just in case Mother Nature decides to surprise you with some unexpected showers or unrelenting sun!

25. Phone Chargers

Forgetting phone chargers is one of the most common mistakes made by campers – don't let it happen to you. Make sure your phones and other electronic devices have plenty of juice throughout your entire journey by bringing along multiple chargers (including car chargers) just in case one breaks down or doesn't work properly.

This way, you won't have any worries about staying connected while on the go!

26. Hammock

A hammock is one of the best accessories you can bring with you on your RV trip. Not only does it provide a comfortable and unique place to relax, but it also takes up very little space in your RV. Plus, having a hammock means that you can easily take advantage of any enjoyable outdoor space without worrying about where you'll sleep or sit.

27. Games

Games are essential for long drives and rainy days spent inside the RV. Bring along some classic board games and card games so that everyone in your group can get in on the fun. Consider investing in some travel-friendly versions of larger board games like chess or checkers if space allows.

28. Books

Books are another great way to pass the time while traveling in an RV. Whether you prefer fiction or nonfiction, make sure to bring something along for yourself (other than this book, of course!) and maybe even a couple extra books for others. Reading a book is a great way to unwind after a long day of exploring, and it's also something that everyone in your group can enjoy together when there aren't any other activities going on.

29. Dish Soap

Dish soap may not seem like an essential item when packing for an RV trip, but trust me — it definitely is! Cooking meals while camping requires dishes and utensils that need to be washed with soap and water after each use — so don't forget this essential item!

30. Toilet Paper

Last but certainly not least (especially to me!): toilet paper! Make sure that you always have enough TP stocked up before leaving on your trip; running out of TP definitely puts a damper on things.

This is especially true if there are no bathrooms nearby, as most campgrounds require visitors to take care of their own waste disposal needs. Honestly, this item is probably number one on my list - so make sure you don't forget to pack some. Make sure you've purchased RV-safe toilet paper so you don't have to worry about clogging delicate pipes.

· · ·

Now, here's my advice to you.

Go through these lists and figure out if there's anything else you want to add. I always find it helpful to envision a typical day of RV camping, going so far as to write down all the activities I might do, starting with the moment I wake up in the morning until I lay my head down on the pillow at night.

What's missing? Do the lists above have everything you might need?

If you think of anything else, write the items down in the margins (or on a separate notepad if you're reading this digitally). Print off the checklists from this chapter to make sure you have everything you need.

After all, you might be able to find a Walmart or convenience store along your travels so you can buy whatever you're missing - but what if you're boondocking? What if you don't have access to modern conveniences? You really don't want to be 100 miles from civilization and realize - yikes - you don't have any toilet paper.

Just think - none of us wants a repeat of the "trip that shall not be mentioned."

Terrified yet? I don't mean to scare you - but a little bit of healthy fear is never a bad thing when it comes to preparedness!

Make your list, check it twice - and don't be like me. Pack the extra TP.

4

WHAT DO I DO UPON ARRIVAL AND DEPARTURE?

 "There's no Wi-Fi in the mountains, but you'll find no better connection."

— ANONYMOUS

When you're planning a trip, you likely put a lot of time into the logistics. Where will you stay? How will you get there? What sorts of attractions will you visit while you're there?

It's fun to plan a trip - and if you're planning on bringing your RV out on the open road, preparation is just as much a part of this experience as it is any other vacation. You need to be prepared!

The great thing about RVing is that you have access to your transportation, meals, and housing - all in one unit! You don't have to worry about those sorts of logistics.

However, you do need to make sure your RV is up to the task. Before you even arrive at your destination, there's work you need to do in order to make sure you can get there without any issues and to make sure you're ready to start camping as soon as you arrive.

Going through the proper steps both prior to and upon arrival and departure with your RV is essential. Not only will it give you peace of mind, but it will also reduce the likelihood of problems popping up when you're on the road.

Remember, there's no Wi-Fi in the mountains - and while you might be headed to a destination that's more metropolitan than backwoods, it's important to prepare ahead of time to make sure you're ready to connect with nature and enjoy your trip once you get there.

Let's take a closer look at what you need to do.

Regular Maintenance Checks Before Any Trip

Maintenance checks before your trip are essential - not only will they give you the peace of mind that everything is as it should be as you're rolling down the open highway, but they can also save you money.

How, you might ask? It's simple. It's much easier to fix or replace damaged parts when you're still at home and close to a repair shop than it will be when you're thousands of miles from home and find yourself with a problem.

These checks will keep you safe on your journey and prevent costly repairs that can disrupt your travels.

Here are a few of the systems and parts we recommend checking before you leave the house - feel free to add other steps as you see fit.

Check On Your Axles, Brakes, Fluids, and Filters

If you can, enlist the help of a mechanic for this first element of RV maintenance. It's a good idea to give your RV a full work-up and inspection if it's the first road trip of the season.

It's important to double-check your manual in this regard, too. Some maintenance is meant to be done only by a certified technician, and completing the work yourself could result in you voiding your warranty.

So, what will this inspection entail?

When prepping your RV for the season, you'll want to grease the axles, adjust the brakes, and check the differential fluid (at a bare minimum). You should also inspect the level of your automotive fluids by looking at dipsticks and reservoirs (these are located under the hood).

Don't skip a thing. You'll want to check the engine oil, brake fluid, power steering fluid, radiator coolant, antifreeze, and transmission fluid.

Even take the time to top off your windshield washer fluid! Whenever I think I'm ready to go after checking my oil, gas, and all other levels, I remember that 100-mile trip on backcountry roads in the dead of winter.

It sounds like a small thing to be worried about, but let me tell you - driving behind a snowplow spreading salt on the roads without any windshield washer fluid was less than ideal and, honestly, downright frightening at some points when passing or pulling over wasn't an option.

Moral of the story - double-check everything. It doesn't hurt to have a few extra jugs of fluid stocked up in your RV, either.

Ideally, you should drain these fluids at the end of the season, but if you didn't do that last year, it's a good idea to completely change everything out so you don't have old oil and fluids lingering around in your RV. Fresh is best!

You should also take the time to check on your filters. Filters don't necessarily need to be replaced unless they're worn. Over time, they become warped, damaged, and worn out from particulate damage.

While the exact location of each filter will vary depending on what kind of RV you have, it's a good idea to check on each one. If it's damaged or extremely dirty, replace it - otherwise, you may be able to simply clean it to get more use out of it.

Here are the air filters you'll want to check on:

- **Fuel filter** - These are often see-through, making it easy for you to see the condition of the filter and the fluid's color. If the filter is not transparent, you will want to look at your engine performance for an idea of whether or not this needs to be replaced (such as poor fuel efficiency and engine stalling). You can find the fuel filter along the fuel line between the engine and the fuel tank (sometimes, it's under the vehicle itself).

- **Oil filter** - The oil filter should be changed every time you change the engine oil. It's attached to the engine block and is relatively easy to find.
- **Cabin air filter** - You may or may not have a cabin air filter in your RV. Check your owner's manual to determine if you have one, and if so, figure out where to find it and change it out.
- **Engine air filter** - Last but not least is the engine air filter. This filter is found inside a piece connected to the engine block. Pay close attention to how this filter is oriented when you take it out; otherwise, it could be tricky to put it back on.

Maintenance is an integral step of caring for your RV, and it's vital that you don't overlook a thing. You don't want to be driving through Death Valley and discover that you're out of coolant.

Pay Attention to the Belts, Wiring, Lights, and the Horn

Another part of your mechanical inspection should involve the belts, hoses, wiring, lights, and the horn. These are components of an RV that are often neglected but are important if you want to keep your motor home running at peak performance.

Take a look at the belts, hoses, and wiring to make sure everything looks functional. While you may need to enlist the help of a professional to inspect and replace these, essentially, you're looking for noticeable damage like holes, cracks, frayed areas, and exposed wires.

Test all of your tail lights, headlights, turn signals, and hazard lights. Again, these are far easier to replace in your hometown than they will be when you're camping in a remote area.

And finally, test the horn. If you have little kids coming with you on the trip, they'll love having this particular job delegated to them! Check to make sure the horn is functional since it's a key aspect of safety while you're out on the road.

Arriving at the Campground

For first-time and experienced RV campers alike, the process of checking in can be daunting. There are a lot of steps to follow, and getting them all right is essential for a successful camping trip. Thankfully, with some simple preparations and a bit of patience, you can ensure that your check-in process goes smoothly. Let's dive into the essentials of RV camping check-in!

Confirm That the GPS Directions Are Correct

Before you leave for your campground, double-check that the directions from your GPS are correct. You probably want to avoid getting lost en route or ending up at an incorrect location! Make sure that you have multiple navigation options available so that if one fails, you can use another as backup.

Register

When you arrive at the campground, look for the registration area. If it's your first time there, it's likely that there will be signs directing you to this area. Depending on where you are located, there may also be someone outside who can assist with finding the registration office or answer any questions you might have about the campground layout or facilities.

Once you have found the registration office, slowly maneuver into the check-in line. Some campgrounds may have designated lanes for different types of vehicles (RV vs. tent camping), so make sure that you are in the correct lane before proceeding further. This also gives you a chance to take in your surroundings and get familiar with how different aspects work at this particular campground.

When it's time to check in, shut off your vehicle and put your dog in a crate if needed. It's important to keep them safe during this process! Grab your wallet, confirmation documents, dog records (if applicable), and snap a picture of the license plate on the way into the office —this is helpful for when it comes time to depart later on down the line!

Once inside, fill out any necessary paperwork and let them know what type of site/campsite amenities/services you require—if they aren't already listed on your confirmation document(s).

They will provide you with a check-in pamphlet with directions to your campsite as well as other relevant information such as gate codes (if applicable), rules and regulations around pets/noise levels/fire safety etc., Wi-Fi password etc.—all essential information for enjoying a comfortable stay!

Get the Lay of the Land

Now it's time to get your bearings and familiarize yourself with the layout of the campground. If needed, determine where the dump station and fresh water fill are located—you may need to use these amenities during your stay. Don't be afraid to ask questions if you have any—the staff are there to help you out. After getting all of your questions answered, it's time for a walk around the grounds.

Once you know where everything is located, take some time to scout out other campsites that catch your eye. This way, when you arrive back at your own campsite after a long day of outdoor activities, you will have an idea of what amenities may be available nearby if needed. It also doesn't hurt to check out any scenic sites within walking distance—they will make for some great photos!

Find Your Site

Make sure that you double-check which campsite was reserved for you beforehand so everything is clear on arrival. Once you find it, jump into your RV and drive slowly toward your designated spot.

If applicable, stop off at both the dump station and fresh water fill before heading directly into your site; this way, these tasks won't need to be done later and can free up more time for activities instead. Later in the book, I'll tell you exactly how to do this so you know the ins and outs of this process.

Finally, if you have a tow vehicle (or "toad"), unhook it from the RV in designated unhook/hookup areas so that it can be used as needed throughout your stay. Not all campsites have these areas (some allow you to just park your car at your site), so pay attention to the instructions at check-in.

Setting Up Camp

This next process can be somewhat tedious, but it's essential when it comes to enjoying the rest of your stay - now you've got to set up camp!

Pull Into Your Site

Locate the designated site number for your campsite. Once you have located it, take a moment to step outside of your vehicle and examine the area you will be backing into to identify any obstacles you may not have seen from inside the cabin.

If you have a spotter or another person to help guide you when backing in, have them examine the space with you as well. Having a spotter is one of the best pieces of advice I can give you on backing in with an RV, even if it's just another camper on site willing to help you. Some people also bring two-way radios to communicate with their spotter when backing in. If you are driving a towed camper, back up slowly and turn your wheel all the way in the direction of where you want to go—this will help ensure that you don't overshoot or misalign while backing up.

If there's a marked parking spot, this should be relatively easy. Some campsites take the guesswork out of the equation and use paint or marking materials to indicate where to back your rig in so that you can hook up appropriately.

If the campsite doesn't have the spot marked, you'll want to pay attention to how the utilities are labeled and laid out. Usually, you'll be parking your RV on a concrete pad. Often, the separate utilities (like black water hookup, fresh water hookup, electricity, etc.) are marked with written labels or color-coded. It's different everywhere, so pay attention to the instructions when you check-in.

And if you're boondocking or camping at a more primitive site, there might not be hookups at all. If there are designated parking spots for your campsite, park there - otherwise, just keep an eye out for hazards as you pull in. Since you won't be hooking up to any utilities, you can be a bit more liberal in choosing where to park.

Once parked on-site, shut off the vehicle and get ready for some exploring!

Do Some Exploring

Once settled into your campsite, do a walk around to familiarize yourself with the area. Take note of any surrounding wildlife or unique terrain features nearby. At the same time, do a walk-through of your campsite so that you can assess what amenities are available (e.g., picnic tables, fire pits).

This is also a good time to survey any potential hazards, such as large rocks or tree roots that could cause tripping hazards when navigating around camp after dark.

Park the RV

Make sure that the RV is parked level and secure. This step will ensure that your camping experience is as comfortable as possible by making sure that everything inside stays level while also limiting the likelihood of accidents (like roll-aways). It will also prevent the entire weight of the vehicle from sitting flat on the tires, which isn't necessarily a bad thing, but if done repeatedly over time, can wear out the rubber on your tires.

The leveling process will differ slightly for a towable versus a motorized RV, but in general, you'll want to have a bubble level, leveling blocks, wheel chocks, and jack pads.

If you have a towable RV, start by placing the wheel chocks on either side of the tires to stabilize the camper. Then, for either type of RV, place the bubble level on a flat surface such as the floor or a tabletop to gauge how level you are, both front to back and left to right. Don't forget to set the parking brake each time you leave the vehicle!

If the bubble level shows the RV is tilted one way or another, use leveling blocks to adjust accordingly until the RV is level in each direction. The best way to do this is to set up the leveling blocks in a pyramid or ramp shape and slowly, carefully drive up the blocks as needed. It's best to use as few blocks as possible to achieve a level surface.

After you're happy with the way your RV is leveled, place those final wheel chocks around any unblocked tires. If you're using a towable RV, unhitch the RV from your vehicle and lower your tailgate so you can safely pull the vehicle away.

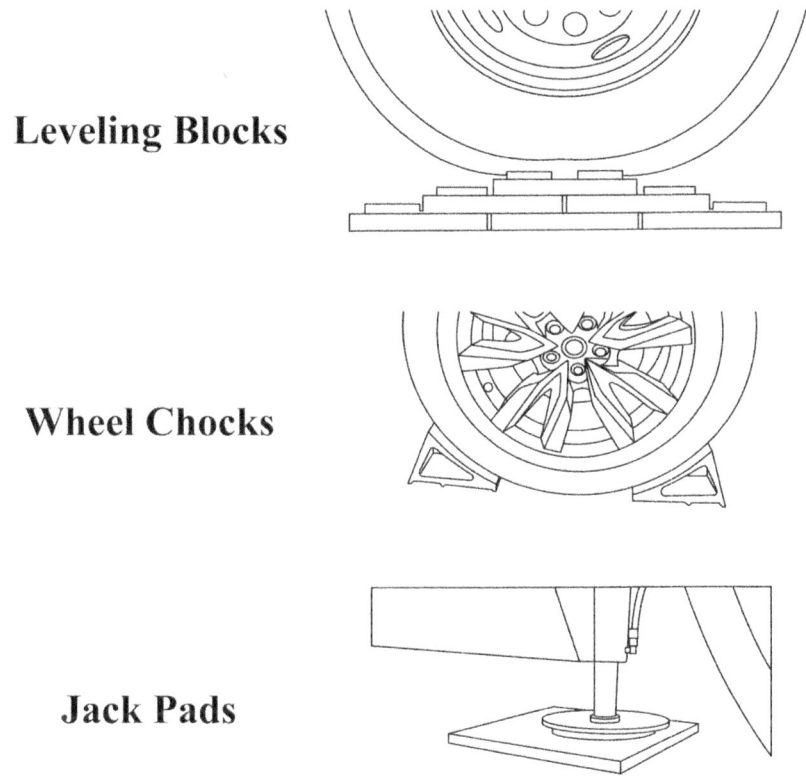

Leveling Blocks

Wheel Chocks

Jack Pads

Diagram showing (from top to bottom) six leveling blocks under a tire, two wheel chocks around a tire, and one jack pad under an RV stabilizing jack.

Finally, lower your stabilizing jacks and place jack pads underneath to prevent damage to the ground below (these are notorious for damaging asphalt!). You may also want to put down a few tarps or boards beneath your wheels and jacks for extra protection from moisture or insects. Once everything looks good, you can deploy steps and handrails as needed.

To expand your living space even further, extend all slide-outs on your rig so that you maximize available living space for all occupants. I recommend waiting to pull out slide-outs until after hooking up sewer and electric lines in case the slide-outs obstruct the path to your campground connections. If the battery for your chassis has a disconnect switch (which many Class-A motorhomes have), make sure that it is disconnected prior to hooking up electrical power from shore power supplies at campground sites with electricity hookups (30 amp, 50 amp, etc.)

It's important to test the voltage of electricity with a voltmeter before hooking up electrical power from shore power supplies at campground sites with electricity hookup services such as 30-amp & 50-amp services.

This step is essential in order to ensure proper voltage levels are present before connecting any electrical appliances and devices inside an RV that might get damaged due to incorrect voltage levels supplied by a campground site's electric power supply service connection point.

Get Connected

Next, you'll want to "plug in" your RV. Make sure that the receptacle matches your amperage requirements. Most RVs require 30- or 50-amp electrical service. To figure out which one yours is, look at the plug. 30-amp plugs will have three prongs, while 50-amp plugs have four. Next to your power outlet, you may see a warning label indicating the recommended amperage for your unit - if you're not sure what kind of power service your campground provides, ask the campground when you check in or look at the electrical stand (it will often be labeled).

To plug in, locate your power cord on the RV. This is typically found coiled up in the driver's side compartment where your holding tank outlets are. Make sure your RV is stabilized, blocked, and leveled before you plug in, and that the cord will reach.

Then, turn on the breaker switch near the electric box and check to ensure that it's working by turning on lights or appliances. You'll also want to run the fridge for at least an hour before putting food inside so it has time to cool down.

Once your electricity is hooked up, it's time to get your water and sewer hoses connected. Some campsites provide water via city water (an external water source), while others get water from a well. This isn't super important to know before you make your reservation; the hookup process is the same. You're hooking the RV up to an externally pressurized water spigot, simple as that.

Start by attaching your white water hose (which means it's drinking water safe, also referred to as a potable water hose) to both the camp supply and your RV. Most of the time, the water connection is found on the driver's side exterior wall. It will be a threaded connection into which you can screw the water hose.

The spigot to attach this hose should be located near the electric and sewer connections. Install your pressure regulator by screwing the female end of the regulator onto the spigot, then attach your hose to the male end. If you have an inline filter that you'd like to use (which will reduce the number of chemicals and contaminants that enter your RV's plumbing), you can attach this now, too. Not mandatory, but a good step if you aren't sure where the water is coming from.

Once you have your pressure regulator and filter in place, open up one of the faucets in your kitchen sink inside the RV. Turn it on about halfway (not full blast). This will help reduce issues with water pressure if the regulator happens to malfunction.

Turn on the supply of water and check that it's flowing into your RV properly. Check your faucets for good pressure, and make sure water isn't coming out of any connection points. If it is, shut the water off and check the O-rings for wear and tear (or for poor threading - if you've misaligned any of the hoses or they're screwed on crooked, you might find that there is some leakage).

The last step is to hook up your sewer hose. This is the hose that will connect both your gray water tank and black water tank to a drain outside the RV. "Gray water" is any water from shower drains, kitchen sink drains, dishwasher, etc., while "black water" is actual sewage from your bathroom.

Wear gloves while attaching your sewer hose to the drain outlet at the bottom of your RV.

Before you do anything else, picture this scenario: you're relaxing in your RV after a long day of driving, and you decide to take a nice shower. But as soon as you turn the water on, you notice something's not quite right. Suddenly, you're ankle-deep in murky gray water, and before you know it, the water's overflowing onto the bathroom floor! Not exactly the kind of relaxing experience you had in mind, right?

This nightmare can be avoided with a sewer support system that has a slight slope from the RV downward toward where you're connecting it. You can buy an accordion-style sewer hose support before your trip to guide the flow downward. This ensures that gray water doesn't end up flooding your bathroom or any other part of your RV. Trust me, you'll thank yourself later for taking the time to set up your sewer support system properly.

Make sure that other connections like LPG are working properly too. Turn on the supply of LPG at either the valve of the tank or bottle, depending on what type of connection you have. Check that your water heater bypass isn't in bypass mode so you can enjoy hot showers during the camping season!

To do this, locate the water heater, usually found on the side of your RV. Check for valves that control the flow of water into and out of the heater. Make sure the valve leading into the heater is open, the valve leading out of the heater is also open, and the bypass valve is closed. This ensures that water flows into the heater to be heated up before being released into the RV's plumbing system.

Now, you might be wondering what bypass mode even is. It's basically a way to redirect the flow of water around your water heater so you don't have to fill it with water during the off-season. But, if you forget to switch it off, you won't have any hot water for your showers. Trust me, that's not a mistake you want to make!

If you plan on watching TV while camping, hook up cable TV using a coax cable or raise antennae if available at the campground/RV park. You'll be able to get this information about availability when you check-in.

Finally, put out an RV mat for extra protection against dirt and debris entering the living area of the RV.

Get Comfortable!

Once you have parked your RV in its designated spot and taken care of all of your set-up chores, it's time to get comfortable! Set up chairs and tables around the campsite so that you can relax outside without having to worry about balancing plates on laps or standing while eating dinner.

If possible, try to set up these items near each other but far enough away from your RV so that they won't block any windows or doors. This will give you plenty of room for everyone to move around freely without feeling cramped.

Now, it's time to kick back and relax! What better way to enjoy a camping trip than with some delicious food cooked over an open flame? Fire up the BBQ and have fun grilling burgers, hot dogs, kebabs - whatever takes your fancy.

Sit back and enjoy your meal outdoors with friends and family!

Breaking Down Camp

Before you take off to head to your next destination, there are a few important steps that you should be aware of.

Deal With Your Water System

The first step is to disconnect and drain your fresh water hose. This prevents any water from remaining in the hose, which could freeze if left outside in cold weather. Once disconnected, store the fresh water hose in a secure location where it won't get damaged or lost.

Water filters are helpful for keeping your drinking water clean and safe. However, they need to be drained and stored securely when not in use. To do this, open up the filter housing and remove any debris or sediment that may have collected inside.

In some cases, you'll find filters located underneath the vehicle or in the engine compartment. Other times, they may be located in the interior of the RV, perhaps in a cabinet or behind a panel. It's important to consult your owner's manual or do some research to determine the exact location of your RV's filters to ensure they're functioning properly and being replaced as needed.

Then, flush out any remaining particles with a garden hose, if possible (it's a good idea to tote your own in the RV, but many campsites also have these ready to go for campers to use) before closing the housing back up again. Store the filter somewhere safe so that it doesn't get damaged or lost during transport.

Next up is emptying out all of your tanks — fresh water tank (unless needed later), black water tank, gray water tank — as well as cleaning all of your hoses, including utility water hose and sewer hose.

Emptying the tanks in your RV may seem like a daunting task, but with a little bit of knowledge, it can be a breeze. The first step is to make sure that you have a sewer hose that fits snugly into the RV's sewer connection. Next, put on some gloves and grab a tank wand to thoroughly rinse out the tanks. When it's time to empty the tanks, always start with the black water tank first, as it contains sewage waste. You can then use the second flush from the gray water tank (relatively cleaner) to help clean out any residual waste that couldn't be removed from the black water tank flush.

Again, make sure to wear gloves and close the dump valve before removing the lid to avoid any unpleasant surprises. Once the black water tank is empty, it's time to move on to the gray water tank. Keep the valve closed until it's time to empty the tank, and make sure to fully rinse it out when finished.

When emptying tanks, make sure to do so at designated disposal areas only — never dump waste on public land. These areas can vary in location - some may be located near washrooms or in designated dump stations, while others may be placed in more secluded areas throughout the campground.

Wherever they may be located, using the proper disposal area is not only necessary for the sanitation and overall cleanliness of the campground, but it's also important for the well-being of the environment. So, be sure to ask your campground staff about the location of the disposal area for your RV's tanks during your stay.

As for cleaning hoses, use a mild cleaner to scrub away dirt or grime buildup before storing them securely when finished.

One final note - please don't leave your gray or black water hoses on picnic tables to dry out or even to clean. Not only are they dirty, and this is an unsanitary practice (yes, even after you've cleaned them, some debris can still remain), but it *will* annoy other campers. A better idea is to find another spot to clean your hoses or to bring along a tarp to lay your hoses out on. This helps to eliminate the "yuck factor" for sure and doesn't prevent any potential picnickers from enjoying their meal outdoors!

Disconnect the Power and Utilities

Make sure any appliances are turned off, then unplug all power cords from the outlets. If you have a generator, turn it off and disconnect all power cords from it as well. Finally, disconnect any propane tanks or other accessories that may be connected to the RV.

Get the Rest of the RV Ready to Go (and Cleaned Up)

Once all of the power cords are disconnected, you can start getting the rest of your RV ready for travel. Start by wiping down surfaces inside your RV; this includes countertops, tables, chairs, sinks, showers, and toilets.

Then, empty out any trash cans or containers that may have accumulated during your stay at the campsite. Finally, clean up any debris outside of your rig so that it's ready for travel when you arrive at your next destination. Lock the exterior compartments and doors and stow the folding steps.

When it's time to leave the campsite, double-check that all stairs and slide-outs are closed before you remove the blocks and jacks. This will ensure that everything is secure while you're on the road.

Once everything is secured properly, it's time to hit the road! Before departing though, make sure you do a final walk-through inside and outside of your rig just in case there's anything else that needs attention before setting off on your journey.

And that's all there is to it! It doesn't take long to get your RV back on the road once you're used to the process, but don't get discouraged if it takes you longer than you expect to get rolling the first few times you try it.

In fact, I remember one time, camping with my grandparents, it took us all day to get pulled out of the campsite! It seemed like it was just one thing after the next - and it felt like we'd never get back on the road. Give yourself some grace - you'll be at your next destination in no time.

But to make the process even more seamless, be sure to print out the instructions for arriving and departing that we gave you above. Keep a paper copy of this book handy before embarking on or while on your trip in case you need help.

Not only will this save you valuable time and energy while you're on your trip, but it will also be great to have these on hand (and in paper form) in case you don't have cell reception where you've parked your rig.

EMBRACE THE JOY OF HELPING OTHER RV CAMPERS

Now that we've come to the midpoint of our journey in RV camping preparation, you've learned that you'll sometimes need the helping hand of another camper to get to your desired destination (or correctly backed-in to your parking spot).

Which brings me to a question I have for you…

Would you be willing to lend a hand to someone starting their RV camping journey, even if it meant you didn't get any recognition for it?

Imagine this person as someone just like you once were – eager to learn, seeking guidance, but not quite sure where to start.

My goal with writing "RV Camping Guide for Beginners" is to provide an all-inclusive guide to prepare *anyone* to go on a successful RV camping trip even if they have never set foot in an RV before. But the only way to help prepare people is to let them know that this guide is out there.

This is where your help comes in. Many people do judge a book by its cover (and its reviews.) So here's my humble request on behalf of someone out there who needs help getting started on their RV camping journey:

If this book has helped you in any way so far, please consider passing on the same help to that lost, aspiring RVer by leaving a review for this book.

Your act of kindness costs nothing and takes less than a minute but could have a profound impact on someone's life. Your review might…

…help a family create lasting memories on their RV trips.

…guide a newbie RVer through their first camping experience.

...inspire someone to pursue their dreams of RV travel.

...provide valuable insights for future readers.

To experience the joy of making a difference and truly help someone, all you have to do is...and it'll take less than a minute...leave a review.

Simply scan the QR code below to leave a review:

If the idea of supporting a fellow aspiring RVer resonates with you, I'm delighted to welcome you into the RVing community. You belong here.

I'm thrilled to be able to assist you in achieving your RV camping goals faster and easier than you ever imagined. You'll find valuable insights and tips in the upcoming chapters that I'm excited to share with you.

Thank you sincerely for your support. Now, let's get back to making memories on the road.

- Your friend and guide,

Rain Tucker

5

WHAT ARE COMMON ISSUES I SHOULD BE AWARE OF AND AVOID?

 "Camping rules: Stare at the fire. Listen to the birds. Jump in the lake. Read. Take a nap. Relax. Watch the sunset. Cook over the fire. Breathe the fresh air."

— UNKNOWN

Campfires. Birds. Lakes. Books. Naps. Sunsets. Fresh air. It all sounds pretty magical, doesn't it?

And honestly, it is. RV camping offers all the above experiences - and then some.

But - and this is an important "but" - it will never be perfect.

In all my years of RV camping, I have never - not once - had a completely flawless experience. Things will always go wrong - it's all about how you deal with them that determines whether those mishaps will make or break your trip.

Good preparation is key to preventing and dealing with the vast majority of camping issues. One of the best things you can do is to read up on some of the most common RV camping problems that may arise - which I'll tell you all about below.

That way, you'll not only be able to go into your camping experience with a clear and realistic idea of what could go wrong, but you'll also have an idea of how to fix these problems when they arise.

Let's get started!

Attaching Breakaway Cable to Receiver

For RVs that attach to a tow vehicle, a breakaway switch is a safety device that prevents accidents if your trailer becomes disconnected from the tow vehicle during transit. The switch itself is connected to a cable that must be attached to the tow vehicle. The breakaway cable may look like a thin silver cable or a red accordion-style cable.

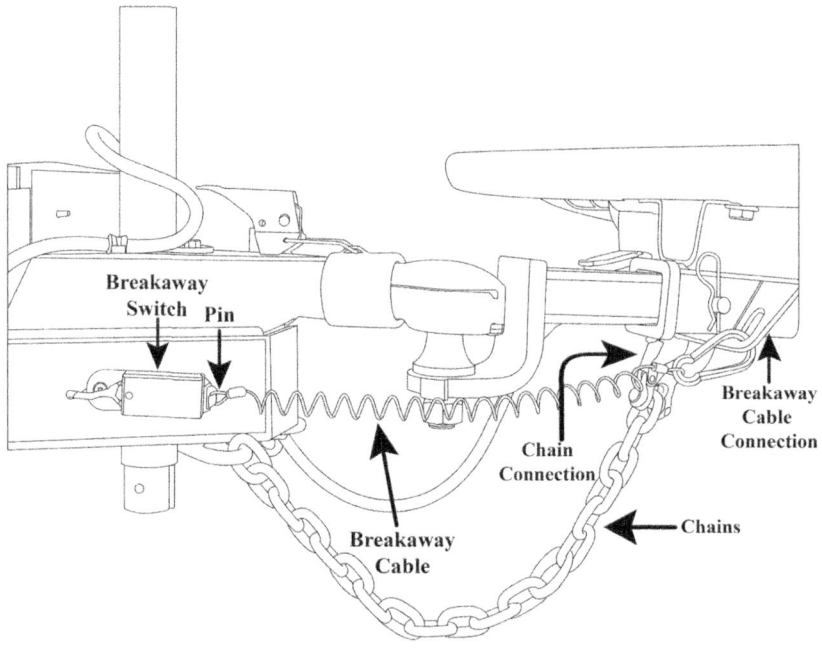

Diagram of connection between RV (left) and tow vehicle (right). Proper placement and connection of breakaway cable, separate from chain connection, is shown.

In the event of a separation, the cable will stretch out until tension is at a maximum, and the pin will be pulled out from the switch, which activates the brakes on the trailer to slow it down and eventually stop it. These switches are powered by 12-volt RV batteries.

It's essential to make sure you properly install your breakaway switch in order for it to work correctly. Many owners attach their cable to their safety chain hooks or ball mount simply because they think those locations are easy to access — but they aren't necessarily safe or legal! I recommend consulting with an expert before installing yours so that you can ensure optimal performance and safety. Keep in mind that you should try to loop your breakaway cable to a connection on your tow vehicle that is different from where your chains are attached. Even better, attach the cable to your tow vehicle and RV frames if possible in case the trailer hitch or receiver on the RV fails.

It's vital that you check all connections before going on any RV camping trip, including inspecting your breakaway cable for any signs of wear or damage that may render it ineffective in case of an emergency situation. Make sure it is securely attached at both ends with less slack than your chains but enough slack to safely make turns and normal maneuvers without pulling the pin out accidentally.

In case something does go wrong, however, and your trailer becomes detached from your tow vehicle while driving, then this pin will be pulled out, and all brakes on the trailer will engage automatically, allowing you to slow down safely without risking an accident from a loose RV going full speed down the highway with no control.

Consider bringing extra pins just in case yours has become worn out or damaged beyond repair during use - this can save you a lot of time and money if something goes wrong while you're out on the road!

Tire Blowouts

When you're out on the open road, the last thing you want to worry about is a tire blowout. But if you own an RV, this is a very real possibility that can happen at any time. Knowing the signs and taking preventive measures can help ensure that your camping trip runs as smoothly as possible - without any unexpected tire blowouts.

It's important to be aware of the signs of wear and tear on your tires. If your vehicle has been running for over six years, it's likely time for a tire replacement.

Pay attention to any signs of bulges or cracks in the sidewalls of your tires - these are warning signs that your tires are due for replacement sooner rather than later. Also, make sure to check the air pressure in your tires regularly (at least once every two weeks). This will ensure that they are properly inflated and able to maintain their structural integrity over long distances. I recommend bringing a portable air compressor with you to make this task more convenient, especially for those longer or more remote journeys where you might really need it.

If you're planning a long-distance trip with your RV, it's best to get all four tires replaced before leaving home. This will help prevent any potential blowouts from occurring mid-trip, which could cause major delays or additional expenses.

It's also important to be aware of how much weight you're carrying in your vehicle and adjust accordingly if needed - too much weight can put unnecessary stress on your tires, leading to a chance of tire blowouts happening while on the road.

Finally, try not to drive faster than necessary - this increases friction between the tire and road surface, which can lead to increased heat buildup within the tire itself - resulting in a higher risk of blowouts happening during sudden stops or turns.

In the unfortunate event that you do experience a blowout, resist your natural urge to hit the brakes. Accelerating just a little bit will help you stay in control of the vehicle rather than swerving in the direction of the blown tire. Once, you've regained control over the vehicle, let the car decelerate naturally and head over to the shoulder in the right-most lane to address the damage.

Leaky Roofs and Windows

Fortunately, this is not an issue I've had to personally deal with - but trust me when I say I've had plenty of fellow camper friends who've had to clean up major messes when their roofs or windows start to drip water into the RV. Not a fun way to spend your vacation, to say the least!

The best way to handle leaky roofs and windows when RV camping is to prevent them from happening in the first place.

Make sure that you inspect your roof for any signs of damage or wear before each trip. Pay special attention to the seals around vents, air conditioners, etc., as these are often the first places where leaks develop.

Also, be sure to check for any missing or loose screws that could cause water damage over time. If you're planning on traveling during the rainy season or in regions known for high levels of rainfall, it's always a good idea to invest in some waterproof sealant or tarpaulins (especially if you have any skylights).

If your roof or windows already have leaks, then there are several steps you can take to fix the problem.

First, try using caulk or silicone sealants around the edges of any windows or vents that seem particularly vulnerable. If this doesn't work, then you may need to replace the entire window or vent cover. You should also consider investing in special roof coatings that are designed specifically for RVs; these coatings will help protect against future leaks as well as help repair existing ones.

Finally, if all else fails, it may be time to call a professional who specializes in fixing leaks on RVs—they can provide more detailed advice about what needs replacing and how best to go about doing so safely and efficiently. Again, it's best to deal with these issues before you hit the road - which is why doing a thorough inspection of your RV before you take off on your next grand adventure is so important.

Toilet Issues

The most common issue when it comes to toilets in RVs (as is likely the case in your home itself!) is clogs. Clogs can be caused by too much waste being flushed down the toilet at once or by foreign objects, such as paper towels or feminine products, getting stuck in the pipes.

If your toilet begins to back up or overflow, don't panic—there are some easy fixes that can help get it flowing again.

If your toilet overflows or backs up, the first step is to shut off the water valve near the base of the toilet. This will stop any additional water from entering the bowl and will help contain any mess that has already been made.

Once the water supply has been turned off, you can then use a plunger to try and dislodge whatever is causing the clog. If this doesn't work, you may need to call a professional plumber for assistance.

The best way to avoid toilet issues while camping in an RV is through regular maintenance and cleaning. Make sure you only flush items that are specifically intended for use in RVs (such as special RV-safe toilet paper), and never flush paper towels or feminine products down your RV's toilets.

Be sure to periodically clean out any residue that may be building up inside your pipes using a special cleaner designed specifically for RVs (look for one labeled RV cleaner - often, these are marketed as being both marine and RV safe). This will help keep your pipes clear of debris and reduce the risk of clogs occurring in the future.

Other Plumbing Issues

One of the most common plumbing issues when RV camping is water pressure dropping off or becoming too high. Low water pressure can be caused by sediment buildup in pipes or a clogged filter. High water pressure can damage pipes and even cause leaks if it goes unchecked for too long. Typically, high water pressure is due to flow issues at the RV site. You can't necessarily change that, but you can adjust your regulator inside the RV.

Your water heater is essential during an RV camping trip—it allows you to shower, wash dishes, and more! This is why it's important to keep an eye out for any problems that may arise with your water heater while you're out camping. One common issue is sediment buildup in the tank that prevents proper heating and circulation; again, this can be addressed by flushing the tank regularly with vinegar or bleach solutions (check with your manual first!).

Another issue could be low pressure due to too much calcium buildup in the pipes; this can be fixed by using pipe descaling products like CLR or boiling hot water down your plumbing system every so often. If you find yourself without hot water, double-check that all valves have been opened properly before calling in a professional plumber. This is a simple solution that you can handle yourself.

Then there's the issue of a sewer line leak. A sewer line leak can be an unpleasant experience for any camper. The smell alone is enough to ruin any camping trip! Sewer line leaks can be caused by age, temperature changes, or simply the wear and tear of being on the road.

If you suspect you have a sewer line leak, check all the connections from your RV to your campsite's hookup area for any signs of leaking. If you don't spot anything, check around your campsite's hookup area and up into your RV's sewage tank itself for any signs of leakage.

Leaking pipes are another common problem when it comes to RV plumbing, as they can cause water damage and mold growth inside your home. To prevent leaks, make sure all fittings are properly tightened before hitting the road, and double-check them after each trip for any signs of wear or deterioration. Also, be sure to inspect your pipes periodically for signs of corrosion or leaks and replace them if necessary before serious damage occurs.

Battery Problems

When you're camping in an RV, it's important to have a reliable power source. Unfortunately, batteries can sometimes fail, leaving you stuck without the power you need.

One of the most common problems with RV batteries is that they are overcharged. This happens when the battery is charged too quickly or left connected to the charger for too long.

An overcharged battery will not last as long as a properly charged one and can cause your other appliances to stop working due to the lack of power. To avoid this problem, make sure your RV battery is always disconnected from the charger once it has been fully charged.

On the other hand, undercharging your battery can also be an issue. This happens when you don't charge your battery often enough, and it isn't receiving enough energy from its source. If you notice your appliances not working or not lasting very long on one charge, try charging your RV battery for longer periods of time than usual before using them again.

Then, there's a deep discharge. Deep discharge occurs when a battery has been discharged beyond its capacity and cannot maintain an adequate voltage level due to sulfation buildup on its plates. To avoid deep discharge problems, never allow your batteries to be deeply discharged during regular use or storage periods; always keep them topped off with an appropriate charging source. Check your battery often while it's in storage (at least once per month but perhaps more often in cold weather) and recharge as needed.

Also, if you plan on storing your RV for long periods of time, it's important that you disconnect any electrical connections from the battery so that no current flows through it while in storage mode.

Another possible cause of battery failure is dirty terminals on your RV battery. Over time, dirt and grime can build up on the terminals and prevent them from making contact with the cable connections properly. To check if this is an issue, clean off any debris or dirt that may be stuck to the terminals before reconnecting them back to their cables and trying again.

AGAIN, this is another chapter of the book that is particularly helpful to have on hand as a paper copy. It's all too easy to say, "ah, I'll just do an internet search if it happens - there are plenty of articles and tutorials out there to help me out!"

And to some extent, that's true. I can't tell you how many times I've leaned on a YouTube tutorial to help me figure out how to diagnose a toilet that won't flush or how to stop a leak in the roof.

However, the internet is unreliable - even in places that have a good connection (I'm looking at you, people who love those urban camping experiences!), you may have a device that doesn't want to cooperate, or you might just be unable to find what you're looking for exactly when you need it.

Therefore, it's always best to print and save these diagnostic tips and advice so you have the help you need when you need it - rather than taking valuable time away from your camping trip going down the Google rabbit hole.

An ounce of prevention is worth a pound of cure - and when you can't prevent it from happening, having the cure already loaded up is the next best thing.

6

HOW CAN I STAY ON BUDGET WHILE RV CAMPING?

 "You can't buy happiness...but you can buy an RV, and that's pretty close."

— UNKNOWN

They say money doesn't buy happiness- which is a good thing because I've never had much of that.

Fortunately, one doesn't have to be a millionaire in order to enjoy the great outdoors.

Case in point:

Earlier in this book, I shared a mildly traumatizing story with you about running out of toilet paper (and possibly contracting giardia - who knows - maybe we should have gone to the doctor?) in the middle of nowhere during a (failed) boondocking experience with my family.

Hopefully, that didn't completely deter you from the idea of RV camping - but if you're still reading, I'm glad you're hanging in there! Hopefully, my mishaps have proven to be at least mildly entertaining (and if not, I hope you're not shaking your head too much at me.)

Horrible #2 experience aside, I will say that boondocking is actually an enjoyable and economical way to enjoy everything that RV camping has to offer. In fact, it's one of the best ways to save money while you're RV camping.

Wait - save money? On vacation? That's a thing?

Absolutely. It's what has allowed me to continue RV camping all these years.

I love the allure of spending time in nature, and I love the fact that it's (mostly) free. While you could definitely spend thousands of dollars each trip, purchasing elaborate, extravagant meals and going on high-dollar outings, the reality is that RV camping is just what you make it.

Boondocking, for example, is a great way to camp without having to worry about astronomical campground fees. You simply park it where you please (within reason, of course- you have to do this in a place where it's actually allowed).

But boondocking isn't the only way to save some cash. Let's take a closer look at how you can enjoy a budget-friendly camping trip!

Prepare Meals Ahead of Time

Going on an RV camping trip can be a great way to get away from it all and enjoy some quality time with your family or friends. Unfortunately, it can also quickly become expensive if you're not careful about budgeting for meals. One way to stay on budget is to prepare meals ahead of time.

The first step in preparing meals ahead of time is to plan what meals you will be making while on your RV camping trip. To do this, decide how many days you will be camping and the number of meals you want to eat each day.

Once you have that figured out, look up recipes that fit within your budget and create a grocery list based on the ingredients needed for those recipes. When shopping, stick to the list as much as possible so that you don't overspend. If you can, shop at stores where buying in bulk can help save money.

Once all the ingredients are purchased, it's time to start prepping the food! If you're making something like chili or stew, consider cooking them ahead of time and then freezing them until they're ready for use during the trip. This will also give them enough time for all the flavors to marry together and make it even tastier when you eat it on your trip!

You may also want to cook up some snacks, like hard-boiled eggs or pre-made sandwiches, so they are ready when hunger strikes during the drive. Make sure everything is properly stored in airtight containers before leaving home so that nothing gets spoiled while traveling.

Join RV Clubs

RV clubs often offer members discounted rates when they stay at various campsites. This means that you will be able to enjoy all the comforts of home while saving quite a bit of money on your camping trips! Many RV clubs also offer discounts on services such as gas and supplies.

You can often save as much as 50% or more off your nightly rates just by showing your membership card at check-in.

In addition to discounted rates, members of RV clubs are often eligible for exclusive benefits such as access to exclusive campsites that non-members cannot access or special events and activities organized by the club.

Many clubs also offer their members valuable advice on how to make their camping experience more enjoyable and cost-effective. Members may even find themselves becoming part of a larger network of like-minded campers who share tips and stories about their favorite places to camp!

Of course, it's also important to remember that joining an RV club is a great way to meet new people who share your love for camping! You will have the opportunity to meet other campers who may have similar interests or experiences as you, which can lead to new opportunities down the road. Who knows? Maybe you'll even make some new friends in the process!

There are dozens of savings clubs you can join as an RVer, but some of the most popular include:

1. Good Sam
2. Harvest Hosts
3. Boondockers Welcome
4. Escapees RV Club
5. Passport America

Plan Free Outdoor Outings and Activities

From exploring new trails to visiting local attractions, there are all kinds of free outdoor outings that will keep your wallet happy while ensuring you have an incredible time.

One of the best ways to explore a new area is by taking advantage of its parks and trails. This is especially true for those who love hiking or biking—not only are trails and parks great for exercise, but they also offer stunning views that you won't get from just driving around town. Just remember to check park guidelines before setting out—some may require permits or have specific rules about dogs, camping, etc.

Another great way to save money on your next RVing adventure is by attending local events in the area. Many towns host weekly farmer's markets or art shows that can be a great way to meet locals and get a feel for the area while saving some cash.

Plus, most events like this are free or very inexpensive, so it's easy to fit them into any budget.

If you're looking for something more serene than bustling city events, why not try fishing? Many lakes and rivers are open to fishing without licenses during certain months of the year or throughout certain times of day —just be sure to check local regulations before casting your line! You might even luck out and catch dinner for the night!

Plan for Bad Weather

When going camping in an RV, it's important to be prepared for all types of weather. Rainy days can ruin your plans if you don't have the right activities to keep you and the family busy, but that doesn't mean you need to break the bank in order to have fun indoors.

One way to make rainy days fun is by playing indoor games with family or friends. Board games, card games, puzzles, or any other type of game can provide hours of entertainment without breaking the bank.

Many board games and card game sets are available at discount stores such as Walmart and Target for under $20.

For those who prefer more active games, consider investing in a ping-pong tabletop or indoor mini-golf set – both come in versions that won't take up too much space but still provide tons of fun.

Everyone loves a good movie night! With streaming services like Netflix and Hulu offering hundreds of movies online, there's something for everyone. Some streaming services even offer free access, so you don't need to pay for an account just for one night's entertainment.

If you have kids, consider investing in a DVD player or Blu-Ray player so they can watch their favorite cartoons or movies even when it rains outside or you don't have internet service for streaming.

Rainy days are also great opportunities to get creative with art projects! You can pick up craft kits at most dollar stores; there are usually several choices ranging from simple coloring books and sticker sheets to more complex DIY projects such as painting kits and jewelry-making kits. These projects provide hours of entertainment while encouraging creativity among kids (and adults!).

Try Boondocking

Boondocking is a term for camping without hookups, which means you don't pay for campsite fees or electricity. It also means you're camping outside of established campgrounds with no hookups (water, electric, sewage). It can be a great way to save money and explore more remote areas, but there are some important lessons to learn before you embark on your first boondocking adventure.

This type of camping can be done on public land or private property and usually requires a permit or fee (but almost always one that is lower in price than those of regular campgrounds). Most people who enjoy boondocking stay in their RVs or travel trailers since these vehicles are designed to run on 12-volt batteries that can be charged with solar panels or generators.

Most boondockers feel safe when they are out in the wilderness. However, it's always important to take safety precautions when sleeping away from civilization. Make sure you have a good GPS system so you know where you are going and that you have plenty of fuel in case of emergencies.

Also, make sure your vehicle has plenty of supplies, such as food and water, in case you get stranded somewhere without cell phone reception.

There are a few steps involved when it comes to setting up your own boondocks spot. First, research different locations where you might want to stay. Make sure the area has access to clean water sources if possible so that you don't have to bring all of your own supplies with you each time.

Next, find out what kind of permits or fees might be required in order to legally camp in certain areas. Finally, make sure all of your RV systems are working properly before hitting the road – resources like power sources (batteries/generators), plumbing systems (drainage hoses/water filters), and cooking appliances (stoves/grills).

Ultimately, it is possible to spend very little money when RV camping - and still have great experiences. You just have to prepare ahead of time!

7

HOW DO I WINTERIZE OR STORE MY RV?

 "To appreciate the beauty of a snowflake, it is necessary to stand out in the cold."

— ARISTOTLE

Back in my younger days of solo RVing, I made a lot of rookie mistakes once my grandparents weren't taking the lead on my RV camping trips anymore. I had the typical young adult attitude of, "I know everything, and I'll be fine all on my own."

Besides, I had been RVing with my grandparents my whole life, so I was experienced at this. What was the worst that could really go wrong on any of my trips?

I had ventured out on (what was supposed to be) a quick, peaceful weekend trip to disconnect and see some nighttime stars in late autumn.

Of course, that overconfident and underprepared attitude came to bite me in the rear when I learned firsthand about some critical preparation steps my grandparents were taking behind the scenes before I would join them on some of our colder RV adventures.

Although I had been prepared with warm clothes and gear, I assumed that my RV was tough enough to handle harsh winter weather. Unexpectedly, the temperatures dropped significantly, and after only one night, I felt the consequences of my assumption.

My pipes had frozen, causing all kinds of damage. The sinks and toilets were unusable, and to make matters worse, I was miles away from the nearest town.

I was completely stranded and had no choice but to face the cold weather and try to address the issues myself. Thankfully, I had one portable heater with me to thaw the pipes out. It worked even though it was a tedious process (it took hours!), but I was still left with damaged pipes due to the water expanding as it froze into ice.

The whole ordeal was frustrating, exhausting, and very costly. Even so, one positive thing did come out of the experience; it gave me a huge wake-up call that I would need to fully winterize my RV for the first season of winter storage or take measures of preparation if I decided to continue RVing in the winter.

Needless to say, I was much more diligent about prepping adequately for camping trips after that experience, and hopefully, you will be too after hearing the story.

Winterizing your RV is easier and much cheaper than having to make urgent repairs in the middle of winter. By winterizing your RV, you protect your motorhome from damage and ensure that it remains in perfect condition for the season ahead. It keeps the pipes from freezing, which can cause cracks, leaks, and even lead to flooding.

Plus, it protects your RV's exterior and seals from the harsh winter elements, preventing any damage or leaks.

That winter, I definitely wasn't seeing the beauty of the winter season. After my pipes froze, every snowflake that fell reminded me of my mistake. But clearly, this mistake taught me a valuable lesson. It showed me that in order to fully enjoy the beauty of a snowflake - or of winter RVing - you need to stand out in the cold. You need to make a mistake here or there to realize what needs to be done.

As Aristotle said, to appreciate the beauty of a snowflake, it is necessary to stand out in the cold. However, we must also be prepared and take care of our RVs to ensure they remain in great condition during the winter season.

Winterizing your RV not only helps prevent damage but also saves time and money on repairs. Fortunately, it's easier to do than you might think. Here's what you need to know!

Winterizing Your RV

Winterizing your RV might seem like a daunting task, but it's worth it in the long run. With proper winterization, your RV will be protected, and you'll save yourself money on costly repairs in the spring.

Needed Tools

One of the most important tools required to winterize your RV is antifreeze. This will help protect your plumbing system against freezing temperatures.

Another essential tool to have in your RV during winter is a propane tank. This will provide reliable heat during the cold months. Make sure the tank is at least half full to ensure sufficient heating power. Use propane space heaters to warm the interior of the RV. These heaters are portable, efficient, and easy to use.

It might surprise you to hear that humidity can be an issue during the winter months, when humidity is naturally lower outside. However, inside a sealed unit like an RV, humidity levels can get quite high. This can cause moisture to build up inside your RV, which can lead to mold and mildew growth. That's why it's important to have a dehumidifier. It helps to reduce the levels of moisture in the RV's interior, keeping it dry and comfortable. Dehumidifiers are available in different sizes, depending on the size of your RV.

One of the most important steps to take when winterizing an RV is insulating it correctly. Insulation helps keep cold air outside and warm air inside the RV. Effective insulation helps reduce heat loss, which means you will have to spend less time and money on heating your RV during the winter months. Make sure to insulate your RV's windows, doors, and other spaces prone to air leaks.

Snow can pile up fast during winter, especially if you're traveling to areas with heavy snowfall. A snow shovel will come in handy when clearing snow from the RV's entrance, steps, and other areas. A snow brush is great for clearing snow off the RV's roof and windows.

There are a few other tools and pieces of equipment you'll need along the way, too, but the items listed above are undoubtedly the most important, so stock up before you get started.

The Steps

As the seasons change, it's important to make sure that your RV is ready for the colder months. Winterizing your RV will not only help prevent damage, but it can also save you money by preserving the life of your vehicle. Here's what needs to be done.

1. Drain and Flush Black and Gray Water

The first step in winterizing your RV is to drain and flush the black and gray water tanks. As you may recall, the black water tank is for sewage waste, while the gray water tank is for shower, sink, and washing machine waste.

Both of these tanks can freeze and cause damage to your RV, which is why it's important to fully drain them. Once they are drained, flush them out with a tank flusher to remove any remaining waste.

2. Drain and Flush Water Heater

Next, you'll want to drain and flush your RV's water heater. This step is important because if any remaining water is left in the heater, it can freeze and cause damage.

First, turn off the power or gas to the water heater.

Then, open the pressure relief valve and carefully remove the drain plug. After draining the water out, close the valve and replace the drain plug. Fill the tank with a water heater bypass kit that you can purchase from an RV store.

This will keep water from filling up the heater and prevent potential damage over the winter.

3. Bypass the Water Heater

Before you completely drain your RV's fresh water system, bypass the water heater. This is an important step that can prevent damage to your water heater when it is not in use. You can do this by locating the bypass valve and turning it according to the instructions.

By doing this, you can bypass the water heater and allow antifreeze to run through the rest of the system without filling up and potentially causing damage to the heater.

4. Drain the Fresh Tank and Low Point Drains

Similar to the black and gray water tanks, it's important to fully drain your fresh tank and low point drains. The fresh tank holds the water you use for drinking and cleaning, while the low point drains remove water from your RV's plumbing.

By draining them fully, you can prevent any water from freezing and damaging your RV. If you are unsure how to drain these tanks, refer to your RV's owner manual for instructions. In general, you will need to first make sure that you have a hose that is long enough to reach your RV's sewer system. You also need to make sure that the valve on the black and gray water tanks is fully closed.

Connect your sewer hose to your RV's sewer system and then to the dump station. Once you have ensured that everything is secured, open the valve on your black water tank. The black water will then flow out of the tank and into the dump station. You will know that the tank is empty when no more liquid flows from the hose.

After draining the black water tank, you can move on to the gray water tank. The gray water tank contains less dirty water than the black water tank, but it still needs to be emptied to avoid unpleasant odors. To drain the gray water tank, repeat the same process as for the black water tank. Connect the sewer hose to the gray tank valve and the dump station, and open the valve.

After you have successfully completed the previous steps, you can close the valves on your black and gray water tanks. Remove the sewer hose and stow it away. Rinse and sanitize the hose to ensure that it is clean and safe for use.

5. Find the Water Pump

Next, you will need to locate your RV's water pump to prepare it for winter. The water pump is responsible for pumping fresh water throughout your RV, and it can be damaged by freezing water during winter.

To winterize your water pump, turn it off and disconnect the intake hose. You can use a hand pump kit, connect it to the intake hose, and pump antifreeze through the system. This step will protect your RV from any freeze damage, and it's a must-do for winterization.

6. Open the External Faucets/Valves

Open all external faucets and valves to drain fully to prevent any water from getting stuck in the lines, which will turn into ice and end up causing damage due to expansion. Don't forget to detach and coil up the hoses to avoid any damage or cracking.

7. Open the Internal Faucets, Showers, and Toilets

Open all faucets and showers on the inside of the RV. Once this is done, locate the low point drain and open it to let any remaining water out. Don't forget to clear the toilet, too. The goal here is to ensure that any leftover fluid is out of the system before the winter chill sets in.

8. Pour Antifreeze Down P-Traps

After draining the water from the system, it's time to add antifreeze. To do this, connect a hose to the antifreeze inlet and place the other end into a jug of non-toxic RV antifreeze.

Turn on your water pump and run each faucet and shower while your system is filled with antifreeze. Don't forget the outside shower and toilet, as they require the antifreeze treatment as well.

9. Remove Any Food Items

Make sure you remove any food items that are inside, especially if you won't be using them for an extended period. Doing this ensures that these items won't spoil and attract pests that could damage your RV.

10. Turn Off or Unplug Any Power-Draining Devices

Before you lock up your RV for the winter, ensure any power-consuming devices are unplugged or turned off. Doing so will help preserve the battery life and protect the devices from getting damaged during storage.

11. Switch the Battery Disconnect Switch to Store

The first step is to disconnect your RV's battery. Since winter storage is usually extended, you don't want to risk losing power or damaging the battery. Follow your manufacturer's recommendations for maintaining your battery, but make sure that you switch the battery disconnect to store.

12. Turn Off the Main Liquid Propane Supply Valve

Before you put your RV in storage, make sure that you turn off the main propane supply valve. This will prevent any propane leaks or accidents that might occur. Also, it's a good idea to remove your propane tanks and store them in a well-ventilated area.

13. Turn Off and Clean Out the Refrigerator

Cleaning out the refrigerator and turning it off is essential. You don't want to risk having anything spoil while in storage. Use a towel to keep the door slightly open for air circulation. Be sure to dry the interior of the refrigerator thoroughly before shutting the door.

14. Use Cordless Dehumidifiers

One of the most important steps in winterizing your RV is preventing mold and mildew buildup. Using cordless dehumidifiers inside your RV will help to eliminate unwanted moisture in the air.

These rechargeable dehumidifiers are silent and easy to use. You can place them in closets, cabinets, and other areas where moisture can accumulate.

15. Cover Your Tires

If you store your RV outside, it's essential to cover your tires. It's essential to protect your tires from the elements like the sun, which can cause the rubber to deteriorate. Sun-damaged tires can cause blowouts when the vehicle is driven. A good tire cover will help to prevent any damage from occurring.

16. Put a Mouse Repellent Inside

Mice and other rodents are attracted to the warmth of an RV, so be sure to keep them out by putting a mouse repellent inside. Fresh Cab is a popular choice, as are mouse traps. Make sure to check inside the RV every so often during winter storage to ensure that no unwanted guests have taken up residence.

17. Keep the Cabinets Open

One often overlooked step of winterizing an RV is to keep the cabinets open. This not only provides better airflow to prevent mold and mildew but also allows for better circulation throughout the RV. Keeping the cabinets open will make it easier to regulate the interior temperature, too.

18. Winterize the Generator (If Applicable)

If your RV has a generator, it's important to winterize it properly. Consult the manufacturer's specifications for your particular model to ensure you follow the right steps. Generally, this will involve draining the oil and gas, then adding a stabilizer to prevent any rust or buildup over the winter months.

Storing Your RV

If you're an RV owner, you know that the end of the camping season doesn't mean the end of maintaining your beloved recreational vehicle. Proper storage is essential to keep your RV in good condition, ready to hit the road when you are.

Whether you're storing your RV for a few months or an extended period, here are some tips to ensure your RV is safe and secure.

1. Choose the Location Wisely

The first step in storing your RV is to choose the right location. Ideally, you need a spot that's dry and secure. A covered storage facility is a great option, but it can be costly. If you're storing your RV outside, make sure it's not under any trees, as falling branches could damage the roof or windows.

Opt for a spot that's level, as an unlevel surface could damage your RV's tires.

2. Deep Clean

Before storing your RV, give it a thorough cleaning both inside and out. You don't want any messes to deal with come spring, but a deep cleaning is also vital to prevent small problems from turning into huge ones.

Scrub the walls, floors, and furniture to remove any dirt and stains that could attract pests.

Clean the kitchen and bathroom, including the refrigerator and stove, to ensure there's no food left behind. Wash the exterior of your RV to remove any grime that could damage the paint or finish.

3. Pest Proof

Pests such as rodents and insects can wreak havoc on your RV during storage. To prevent this, make sure to seal any openings, such as vents or pipes, with mesh screens or foam insulation. On the interior of the RV, use pest repellents, such as Fresh Cab or repellent sprays, to repel mice, rats, and other pests. Use peppermint spray on anything touching the ground outside of the RV, and scatter rubber snakes around the exterior of the vehicle to keep unwanted visitors at bay.

4. Remove Any Food

This point has been mentioned already and is worth mentioning again: Leaving food behind in your RV during storage can lead to a serious pest problem. Just take it from me. Many years ago, in my earlier days of solo RVing, I made the mistake of leaving a few packages of crackers and cereal in the cupboards. When I opened up the RV come spring, I found mice droppings everywhere.

Fortunately, I was able to get rid of them with a few traps, but once you've seen mice (or their droppings) in the RV, there's always the paranoia that you still have unwanted guests posing a health hazard in your home. It's not a problem anybody wants to have, and it's easy enough to avoid.

Make sure to clean out your pantry and refrigerator completely. Remove all the canned goods, crackers, or anything that could attract pests or spoil during storage.

5. Retract All Slides

Retracting all of the slides in your RV is an essential part of storing it properly. Not only does this prevent any potential damage to the slides, but it also helps to keep your RV sealed up tight to keep out any dirt or critters.

6. Drain Fluids

Another important step to avoid costly damage is to drain all of the fluids from your RV. This includes water from the fresh water and holding tanks. You should also make sure to add fuel stabilizer to the gas tank to prevent it from going bad.

7. Cover Up Outside

Keeping your RV covered while it's in storage is a great way to protect it from the elements. This can help to prevent any fading or peeling of the paint, as well as protect the tires from UV damage. Make sure to use a durable, breathable cover to avoid any mold or mildew buildup.

8. Cover Up Inside

Just as important as covering the outside of your RV is covering the inside. This helps to keep any dust or critters from settling in and causing potentially costly damage. Invest in some high-quality covers for all of your furniture, electronics, and appliances to keep them looking and working great.

9. Care for the Tires

Tires are one of the most crucial parts of your RV, and they need to be cared for properly even when it's in storage. Before storing your RV, make sure to inflate the tires to the manufacturer's recommended pressure. You should also make sure to rotate the tires every few months to avoid any flat spots from developing.

10. Tend to the Battery

Another important aspect of storing your RV is taking care of the battery. If left unattended, the battery can lose its charge over time and even cause some potential damage. Make sure to disconnect the battery and keep it stored in a cool, dry place. You can also invest in a battery tender to keep it charged up and ready to go for your next trip.

11. Consider Security Measures

Last but not least, consider taking some extra security measures to keep your RV safe and secure while it's in storage. This can include investing in a good quality lock for the hitch, as well as keeping it stored in a secure storage facility. You can also consider adding an alarm system and installing some motion-activated lights to deter any potential burglars.

Pulling Your RV Out of Storage

Are you ready to take your RV out of storage and hit the road again? It can be exciting to plan your next adventure, but before you do, there are a few things you should do to prepare your RV for the journey.

1. Ready the Battery

The first step in preparing your RV for a road trip is to check the battery. If you disconnected the battery before storing the RV, reconnect it and verify that it is fully charged.

If the battery has died over the off-season, you will need to recharge it before your trip.

If your battery is old and not holding a charge, consider replacing it before your trip. A bad battery can cause problems like having to jump-start your RV or your fridge and lighting not functioning.

2. Remove the Cover

Take off the protective cover that kept your RV safe during the storage period. Inspect the cover for any damage, and if there is none, clean the cover and store it in a dry place.

Give your RV a thorough wash and wax to get rid of any dirt that may have accumulated during storage. A good wash and wax not only makes your RV look clean and shiny but also extends its lifespan by protecting it from the elements.

3. Check the Tires

Check the tire pressure and inflate it up to the RV manufacturer's instructions. In addition, examine the tires for any signs of wear and tear, such as bubbles or cracks.

Ensure that the spare tire is inflated and in good condition and you have all the necessary tools and tire repair kit in case of an emergency.

Remember - tires are the backbone of your RV, and you wouldn't want to find a flat tire on your first day on the road.

4. Bring the RV Home and Plug it In

Before leaving the storage facility, connect your RV to a power source and ensure all electrical connections are secure.

You can use an RV electric extension cord if the power source is a little further away than expected. This allows you to start powering up the fridge and other electrical appliances while inspecting your RV.

Leave your RV in a powered area for a good 24 hours to ensure that everything is functioning well before your trip.

5. Inspect the RV Carefully

Before you hit the road, take the time to thoroughly inspect your RV. Check that all the lights are functional, scan the roof for any damage, and look for any signs of potential leaks in the plumbing or roofing.

Check that all the doors and windows are closing properly, and test out the air conditioning and heating units. This final step may take some time, but it ensures that you can enjoy a safe and hassle-free road trip.

RVing in the Winter

As winter sets in, the urge to take your RV on a trip fades away. However, this shouldn't be the case. Winter creates an entirely new environment, and there's nothing quite like experiencing it in an RV.

Before you hit the road, there are a few things you need to consider to make the trip more enjoyable (and to avoid making the same weather-ignorant mistakes I did, as I described earlier in this chapter!).

Fill Fresh Water Tank - and Use a Heated Water Hose

Make sure your fresh water tank is full before hitting the road in winter. When RVing, you never know where you might stop. You'll want to make sure you have plenty of water for cooking, drinking, and cleaning.

To prevent your water supply from freezing, use a heated water hose. The heated hose keeps the water flowing from the tank to the RV when temperatures drop, preventing them from freezing and damaging the hose.

Fill the Propane Tank

Propane will likely be the primary source of heat in your RV, so ensure your propane tank is full. It's always best to fill up your propane tank the night before the trip to avoid running out of gas. Check the pressure gauge frequently to monitor the propane levels.

You can also carry spare tanks to avoid running out of propane when it's cold outside. There's a joke in our community that propane only runs out in the middle of the night, so if you're doing multiple days and nights outside, make sure you're sufficiently prepared.

Keep the Sewer Hose Off the Ground and Flowing Down

When it comes to the sewer, you don't want your hose to freeze or become clogged. To prevent this potential issue, keep the sewer hose off the ground and flowing down. Use a sewer support to keep the hose elevated and flowing downhill to prevent clogs or freezing. Consider bringing a space heater to keep the valve from freezing up.

Keep Gate Valves Closed and Insulated During Winter RVing

To keep your RV warm, you need to avoid heat loss. Keep the gate valves closed because they're the primary source of heat escaping the RV. Gate valves help maintain the warm air in the RV by stopping cold air from entering.

However, it's also essential to insulate the gate valves using heat tape or insulation to prevent freezing.

Run a 60 Watt Incandescent Light Bulb

When the temperatures drop, you need to be able to keep the RV warm. One way of doing this is by utilizing an incandescent bulb to generate heat. When it's cold, run a 60-watt incandescent bulb in the storage area. The bulb generates enough heat to keep the area above freezing. However, you need to keep an eye on it to avoid mishaps.

Seal Off Sewer Hose Entry (or Entries)

One of the vital steps to take when preparing your RV for the winter is to seal off sewer hose entries. Doing so protects your sewer system from freezing and stops the cold from entering the RV through small openings.

Start by placing a cap on the end of the sewer hose, then disconnect and remove the hose from the RV. Next, insert a plug into the sewer opening and ensure it's tight. Lastly, make sure you've emptied and rinsed out the holding tanks before sealing off the sewer hose.

Use Steel or Brass Wool to Seal Up Small Openings

Sealing your RV's tiny openings using steel or brass wool helps keep the cold out and maintains warmth in your vehicle. The steel or brass wool acts as a barrier, preventing cold air from penetrating your RV through small openings.

Some of these small openings may include plumbing pipes and electrical chases. Be careful and seal off these gaps while keeping a watchful eye out to avoid obstructing necessary air circulation.

Use a Remote Temperature Sensor

Remote temperature sensors help RV enthusiasts save money on propane and electricity bills by reducing energy usage.

By keeping an eye on the RV's interior temperature and controlling the heating system remotely, you can regulate the temperature and avoid the need to keep your RV's heating system running constantly, even when no one is inside.

A smartphone-enabled remote sensor allows you to monitor temperature readings, adjust thermostat settings, and even receive alerts when there are significant temperature fluctuations.

Moisture Control for Winter RV Living

Moisture control is particularly crucial during winter RV trips. This might be confusing at first glance since winter is generally a time of lower humidity. However, snow and rain can turn into moisture inside an RV, since it's an enclosed environment, which can cause wood rot, rust, and mildew. To avoid this, ensure that your RV is adequately ventilated.

Open windows or a vent in the bathroom after showering or cooking to let excess moisture escape. Humidity levels should stay below 40%.

Invest in a dehumidifier or moisture absorbers to help bring down the moisture levels in the air inside the RV.

Use Holding Tank Heating Pads

You don't want your holding tanks to freeze during your winter RV trip. Make sure to invest in holding tank heating pads that are specifically designed for RVs. These pads will keep your holding tanks from freezing and make sure you're able to dispose of waste properly.

Warm Your Bed to Use Less Heat

One of the biggest challenges in RVing during the winter is staying warm at night. You can keep your heating bills low by warming your bed instead of heating the entire RV. Opt for bed warmers or heated blankets to keep you cozy throughout the night.

Insulate RV Windows

Heat can easily escape through windows, which is why it's important to insulate them. There are various window insulation options you can choose from, such as plastic films or bubble wrap. Make sure to cover all windows to keep the cold air out and the warmth in.

Insulate Your Skylight

If your RV has a skylight, you need to make sure it's properly insulated. Skylights can be a major source of heat loss during the winter. You can use skylight insulation kits to cover the skylight and prevent heat from escaping.

Cover AC Units

Most RVs have air conditioning units that won't be used during the winter. It's important to cover the unit with an RV air conditioner cover to prevent drafts and moisture from entering the RV. This will help keep you warm and comfortable inside your RV.

Winter RVing isn't for everyone, but winterizing your RV should be on your to-do list regardless. Whether you plan on storing or actively using your RV during the winter months, being prepared will benefit you immensely now, as well as in the spring. Making sure that all food sources are removed or sealed up tightly will go a long way - as will making sure you've fully winterized the rest of your rig.

8

IS FULL-TIME RV LIVING RIGHT FOR ME?

 "The RV lifestyle is a happy marriage of convenience and constant adventure."

— PREVENTION – VOLUME 40, ISSUES 1-6

Full-time RV living can be an experience quite different from venturing out on the road for 1-2 weeks at a time. Before taking the plunge to sell your house and all of your belongings to become an official full-timer, you should experiment with extended RV trips of 4-6+ months to gain a sense of what it will truly be like.

I also highly recommend talking to actual full-timers on your travels to hear their experiences thus far. You can use your potential interest in becoming a full-timer to strike up conversation when you meet other RVers at campgrounds; ask them if they're full-time, how long they've been doing it and what were the greatest challenges they've faced or changes they've had to make.

Full-time RV living isn't for everyone, but for those who crave a life of adventure and minimalistic living, it could be the perfect fit. While it requires some major adjustments, the benefits of cost savings, flexibility, and a welcoming community make it all worthwhile.

Before making the decision to embrace RV living, it's important to weigh the pros and cons and make an informed decision. Who knows, RV living could be one of the best decisions that you'll ever make!

If you're thinking about making the switch, here are some things to keep in mind.

The RV Lifestyle

Are you tired of living a conventional life in a fixed house? Want to experience something different and go on the adventure of a lifetime? The RV lifestyle is one of the best ways to do that! RV living lets you experience a new level of freedom, travel to beautiful places, meet new people, and enjoy life on the road. But is full-time RV living really for you?

What is the Lifestyle of RV Living Like?

First, let's talk about what living in an RV is like. Many RVers say that it feels like living in a tiny home on wheels. You will have limited space for belongings, so downsizing is a must.

On the other hand, this lifestyle provides you with the opportunity to declutter your life, and it can be an exciting process. You'll have to make unique decisions about what to keep and what to get rid of. The living space in an RV is minimal, but you don't have to live in a cramped space.

There are many creative ways to maximize the limited space of an RV, such as installing slide-outs, which can expand your living area.

Ask yourself if full-time RV living is for you. It's easy to get caught up in the idea of RV living, but it's important to recognize that it's not always a perfect scenario. Think about your lifestyle and whether it would fit with the RV lifestyle. In general, RV living is not for someone who needs a set routine or someone who hates change.

Is Full-Time RV Living for You?

There are some questions you need to ask yourself before you set out on this journey, including:

1. Are you ready to separate from possessions, familiar surroundings, and routines?
2. Are you someone who enjoys new places, new friends, and different experiences?
3. Are you someone who requires stability and consistency in life?
4. How much space do you really need to live comfortably?
5. What about your personal relationships?

These are important questions that will help you decide if RV living is something you can handle for the long term.

Facts and Statistics

According to a study by the Recreational Vehicle Industry Association, about 1 million Americans live in RVs full-time.

This RV lifestyle is a popular trend, especially in today's remote work environment. RV living can be a practical and affordable way to travel for those who work online or who can run their business from anywhere in the world.

You can park your RV in any scenic location you want, be it the beach, mountainous terrain, or a park. Not only will you get to see new places, but you can support small businesses along the way!

Did you know that about 51% of RV owners are younger than 55 - and that many of them work full-time while on the road? They spend an average of four to six months a year traveling, and more than half of RVers take their pets with them.

These figures show that the demographic of RV enthusiasts is diverse - and RV living can be a suitable option for the right people.

Helpful Tips and Tricks

The appeal of full-time RV living is undeniable. The idea of shedding the traditional confines of home and hitting the open road is a dream come true for many.

Whether you're looking to travel for a year or make the RV lifestyle a permanent choice, there are some things you should know before taking the plunge.

Get to Know Your RV

Before you hit the road, get to know your RV. Familiarize yourself with maintenance tasks and take a practice drive. This way, you'll feel more comfortable and prepared for any unexpected issues on the road. Pay particular attention to your rig's tire pressure, oil, and coolant levels.

Overpacked RV tires can easily blow out under the stress of long travels, so it's important to inspect them prior to leaving.

Have Plans and Do Your Research

When it comes to planning, do not under-plan or over-plan. Be flexible in the destinations you visit and how long you stay. But before the trip, have a general idea of your route and your timeline, especially if you are on a fixed income. Research your route so you know what to expect, including gas prices, routes, and RV park locations.

Get Your Domicile and Insurance

It's essential to get a domicile and RV insurance prior to actually hitting the road. Your domicile is the state where you plan on keeping your permanent residency, and this is where you'll register and license your RV. It is important for things like voting, taxes, and residency proof.

Getting RV insurance is vital not only to protect the investment but also to safeguard your travels from unexpected damages and accidents on the road.

Downsize

Downsizing can be challenging, but it's a crucial part of becoming a full-time RVer. Determine what you need and what you don't. Sell, donate, or give away anything you don't need in your RV lifestyle.

Be selective on the items that are important to you and think multi-purposes (a blanket under the sun could also provide shade). A good rule of thumb is if you haven't used it in six months, it's time to let it go.

Make a Checklist

Preparation is important in the RV lifestyle. Create a checklist that includes tasks like checking propane levels, performing engine checks, and sanitizing the RV water system. Make sure to pack in advance for long-term trips. Creating a checklist will help you keep track of everything and avoid any traveling mishaps on the road.

Communication is Key

It's essential to have effective communication between everyone living in the RV and those with whom you come into contact on the road, such as RV park staff.

Create a system to communicate to ensure every task is done, and everyone is on the same page. Having consistent care for your RV and good communication with campground staff will only make the RV lifestyle more enjoyable and less stressful.

Expect the Unexpected

The beauty of RV living is its flexibility. You can choose to move around as much or as little as you like.

However, this also means that you need to be prepared for the unexpected. Make sure to have sufficient emergency funds, keep your vehicle well-maintained, and always be prepared for any weather.

Have a contingency plan in place for when things don't go as planned, such as finding a last-minute spot to park your RV. Planning your route in advance and keeping an eye on weather conditions can also help you avoid potential issues.

Be Flexible and Have Fun

While it's important to plan and prepare for your RV living adventure, don't forget to enjoy the journey. After all, the point of full-time RV living is to have fun and experience new things. Stay open-minded and flexible, go with the flow, and don't let unexpected changes ruin your day.

Try new things, step out of your comfort zone, and explore new places. Take advantage of the freedom that RV living provides, and enjoy the adventure.

Storage Solution Tips

One of the biggest challenges of RV living is limited storage space.

To make the most of your space, invest in storage solutions such as hanging storage pockets, under-bed storage containers, and collapsible items such as chairs and cooking utensils.

Make use of wall-mounted storage space or cabinet organizers to utilize otherwise wasted space. Keep your RV organized and clutter-free, and label everything to make it easier to find what you need quickly.

My favorite tip? Come up with an organizational system and follow it. Make sure everyone is on board with what goes where. The good news is that since you'll have far fewer belongings (you already downsized, remember?), it shouldn't take long for everyone to figure out the routine.

Traveling With Pets

For some, RV living simply wouldn't be complete without their furry companions (as illustrated by the statistics conveyed above!).

While traveling with pets can present some challenges, with the right preparation and planning, it can be a rewarding experience.

Make sure to bring all the necessary supplies, such as food, water, and bedding. Keep your pets on a leash or in a crate while traveling, and consider investing in a GPS tracker for extra peace of mind. Don't forget to check ahead for pet-friendly campgrounds and parks, and remember that some places may have restrictions on certain breeds or sizes.

One of the most helpful tips I can give you when traveling with your pet is to make sure they're as well-trained as possible before you hit the road. A pet who knows basic commands and obeys them will create far less stress for you than one who is all over the place.

RV Living With Kids

RV living with kids can be a rewarding experience that fosters family bonding and teaches kids to fully appreciate the diverse world around them. It's one of the exciting ways to explore the country together and create unforgettable memories.

However, there are a few things RV living parents should keep in mind when hitting the road with their little ones.

Get an RV With a Bunk Room Door

If you're considering RV living with children, it's best to choose an RV model with a designated bunk room, offering privacy and personal space for each child. In addition, you may want to make sure the bunk bed has a door so that during quiet time or after the kids are asleep, you can enjoy adult time without bothering them.

Opt for Space-Saving Toys

It's no surprise that kids like their toys! However, when you are living the RV life, space is often limited.

Choosing space-saving toys is beneficial for both the kids and the parents. Look for toys that encourage kids to engage in imaginative play and creativity, such as art supplies, outdoor games, and puzzles.

Stay Organized

RV living requires organization, and having space-saving storage solutions will help keep things tidy and prevent clutter.

Keep daily essentials in a designated area, and use containers to keep things separate and easy to access. Use hooks to hang towels and clothing, and hang a shoe organizer over the back of your door to store small items.

Teach Kids to Conserve

Conservation is essential when living the RV life, and it's a great opportunity to instill these important values in your children. Teach your kids about our environment, and minimize your use of water, energy, and fuel. Encourage them to turn off the lights, take shorter showers, and avoid leaving the water running while brushing their teeth.

Plan Meals

RV living with children requires meal planning to keep everyone happy and satisfied. Plan meals for the week and prepare in advance, using fresh and easily storable fruits and vegetables. Use non-breakable plates and utensils, and invest in a quality cooler. Don't forget to bring enough snacks to satisfy those hunger pangs and provide a source of energy while on trips.

Slow Down

When RV living with kids, you want to create memories that will last a lifetime, so don't be in a hurry to reach your destination. Take the time to enjoy the scenery, and allow the kids to explore and play. Remember, it's not just about the destination, but the journey as well.

Don't Push it on Travel Days

Travel days can be long and boring for kids, and trying to push through it may lead to tantrums and meltdowns. Take plenty of breaks, and let your kids get out and play or stretch their legs.

This is important not just for little kids (although we definitely found it most helpful when our kids were toddlers and desperately needed those little wiggle breaks!) but also for older kids and teens.

Be mindful about what the experience will be like for everyone. Pack travel bags with games, coloring books, and other activities to keep them entertained in the car.

Separate Kids Now and Then

It can be beneficial to separate children now and then, giving them the opportunity to have some personal space, decompress, and relax. My partner and I try to stop at least once a day, and each of us takes one kid to do a different activity that they want to do. One of us might take our daughter for a walk, while the other might take our son to go fishing. It helps to give each of them their space.

Similarly, you should consider allowing each child to have their own space at different points during the day so they can do their thing and recharge.

Embrace the Mess

Living in an RV can be a little chaotic at times, and things aren't always going to be perfect. The good news is that it's okay!

Let the kids be kids and embrace the mess. It's all part of the experience, and it's what makes RV living with kids so special.

Full-time RV living can be a life-changing experience if done right. Plan ahead, remain flexible, and have fun. Embrace the freedom and adventure that comes with a mobile lifestyle.

Remember to stay organized, make use of storage solutions, and be prepared for the unexpected. Most importantly, don't forget to enjoy every moment of your RV journey. With these tips and tricks, you're sure to have an unforgettable and fulfilling experience on the road.

CONCLUSION

 "Earth and sky, woods and fields, lakes and rivers, the mountains and the sea, are excellent schoolmasters, and teach of us more than we can ever learn from books."

— JOHN LUBBOCK

There's nothing quite like the freedom of hitting the open road in your RV. Going on an adventure, making long-lasting memories with your loved ones, and enjoying the beauty of mother nature are just a few aspects of RV camping that make it so special.

Now that you've finished this book, it's time to reflect on the adventure and figure out which pieces of information will be the most important to take with you on the RV expeditions ahead.

RV camping offers tremendous freedom, which puts us in charge of our itinerary. We can pick up and leave at our convenience, see as much or as little as we want, and decide where we'll park, when we'll sleep, and when we'll travel. It's the ultimate way of traveling on our own terms.

As you may have realized when reading here, you're always young enough to learn new things. You can start enjoying the RV lifestyle even if it's something that's totally new to you. Yes, you may learn by making mistakes or facing some inevitable challenges, but actually "doing" is the only true way to learn.

From enjoying a morning cup of coffee in front of a vibrant pink sunrise to roasting marshmallows with a family of wild squirrels at night, RVing lets you explore new places and sights, providing you with opportunities you would not otherwise have. Over time, you'll gain experience and refine your strategies and ability to troubleshoot problems while on the road.

By taking the time to read this book, you've taken the biggest (and most important!) first leap in becoming a proud RVer. This book has equipped you with all the basics of RV camping and the necessary precautionary steps to take before embarking on the open road. Rest assured that with time and practice, your confidence will grow, and you'll transform into the seasoned RV camper you're aspiring to be.

If you enjoyed reading this book or found it helpful in any way, I encourage you to leave a review so that others can also uncover all the wonders that await in the RV camping lifestyle. Let them know what they'll learn here; after all, RV camping is all about learning new things and exploring uncharted terrain.

So, what's the next step? Take the time to decide which RV you're going to purchase (if you haven't already), and set a date to arrive at your first destination.

Where will your first RV adventure take you?

ON THE ROAD TOGETHER
EMPOWER FELLOW RVERS WITH YOUR REVIEW

Just like planning a trip requires careful consideration, so does choosing the right resources.

If this book has enriched your RVing experience in any way, I invite you to pay it forward by leaving a review to help another future RV camper find this resource.

Simply by leaving your honest opinion of this book on Amazon, you'll show other aspiring RVers where they can find the information they're looking for and ignite their passion for RV travel.

Scan on a phone or tablet to go directly to the page to leave a review.

Thank you for your help. The RV camping community thrives when we share our knowledge – and you're helping to do just that.

BIBLIOGRAPHY

ALEX ON THE MAP. (n.d.). Advantages of owning a travel trailer. Retrieved from https://alexonthemap.com/advantages-of-owning-a-travel-trailer/

BEGIN RV. (n.d.). Pop-up camper definition. Retrieved from https://beginrv.com/pop-up-camper-definition/

CAMPERS INN. (n.d.). RV jargon: Terms and what they mean. Retrieved from https://blog.campersinn.com/blog/rv-jargon-terms-and-what-they-mean

CAMPING WORLD. (n.d.). 100 myths about RVs debunked. Retrieved from https://blog.campingworld.com/learn-to-rv/100-myths-about-rvs-debunked/

CAMPING WORLD. (n.d.). An RV checklist for before your trip. Retrieved from https://blog.campingworld.com/learn-to-rv/an-rv-checklist-for-before-your-trip/

CAMPING WORLD. (n.d.). How to winterize your RV. Retrieved from https://blog.campingworld.com/learn-to-rv/how-to-winterize-your-rv/

CAMPING WORLD. (n.d.). Level your RV right the first time. Retrieved from https://blog.campingworld.com/learn-to-rv/level-your-rv-right-the-first-time/

CAMPING WORLD. (n.d.). Tips for backing your towable RV into your campsite. Retrieved from https://blog.campingworld.com/learn-to-rv/tips-for-backing-your-towable-rv-into-your-campsite/

GOOD SAM. (n.d.). Tips for taking your RV out of winter storage. Retrieved from https://blog.goodsam.com/tips-for-taking-your-rv-out-of-winter-storage/

BUCARS RV. (n.d.). The history of RVs. Retrieved from https://bucarsrv.com/learning-centre/camping/history-of-rvs/

CAMP ADDICT. (n.d.). Deadly towing mistake. Retrieved from https://campaddict.com/rv-living/rv-safety/deadly-towing-mistake/

CAMPER FAQS. (n.d.). How much is a pop-up camper? Retrieved from https://camperfaqs.com/how-much-is-a-pop-up-camper#:

CAMPER REPORT. (n.d.). How much is a fifth wheel? Retrieved from https://camperreport.com/how-much-is-a-fifth-wheel/#:~:text=Fifth%20wheel%20prices%20for%202022,fifth%20wheel%20offerings%20from%20manufacturers

CS GINGER. (n.d.). RV kitchen accessories. Retrieved from https://csginger.com/rv-kitchen-accessories/

DRIVIN' VIBIN'. (n.d.). RV roof leaking. Retrieved from https://drivinvibin.com/2022/02/28/rv-roof-leaking/

DRIVIN' VIBIN'. (n.d.). RV plumbing. Retrieved from https://drivinvibin.com/2022/03/07/rv-plumbing/

EXPEDITION MOTORHOMES. (n.d.). What is the difference between Class A, B, C motorhomes? Retrieved from https://expeditionmotorhomes.com/what-is-the-difference-between-class-a-b-c-motorhomes/#:

GLAMPER LIFE. (n.d.). RV bathroom essentials. Retrieved from https://glamperlife.com/rv-bathroom-essentials/

CAMPENDIUM. (n.d.). What is boondocking? Retrieved from https://go.campendium.com/what-is-boondocking/

KOA. (n.d.). Live in an RV full time. Retrieved from https://koa.com/blog/live-in-an-rv-full-time/

LIFE ON ROUTE. (n.d.). 6 reasons your RV battery keeps dying. Retrieved from https://lifeonroute.com/6-reasons-your-rv-battery-keeps-dying/

LIVIN' LIFE WITH LORI. (n.d.). The best RV kitchen and pantry must-haves for your RV. Retrieved from https://livinlifewithlori.com/the-best-rv-kitchen-and-pantry-must-haves-for-your-rv/

NORTHWEST RVING. (n.d.). 10 favorite travel toiletries for your RV. Retrieved from https://northwestrving.com/10-favorite-travel-toiletries-for-your-rv

OUTDOOR TROOP. (n.d.). 21 pros and cons of a Class C RV. Retrieved from https://outdoortroop.com/21-pros-and-cons-of-a-class-c-rv/

PECAN PARK. (n.d.). Stocking the basics in your RV kitchen. Retrieved from https://pecanpark.com/stocking-the-basics-in-your-rv-kitchen/

ROADTRIPPERS. (n.d.). How to boondock. Retrieved from https://roadtrippers.com/magazine/how-to-boondock/

RV DEFENDER. (n.d.). RV tire blowout damage repair. Retrieved from https://rv-defender.com/rv-tire-blowout-damage-repair/

RV ROAD TRIPS. (n.d.). Repair water line in RV. Retrieved from https://rv-roadtrips.thefuntimesguide.com/repair_water_line/

RV BLOGGER. (n.d.). Avoid RV tire blowouts. Retrieved from https://rvblogger.com/blog/avoid-rv-tire-blowouts/

RV BLOGGER. (n.d.). How much does a Class C RV cost? Retrieved from https://rvblogger.com/blog/how-much-does-class-c-rv-cost/#:

RVING IS BEING. (n.d.). RV arrival and set-up checklist. Retrieved from https://rvingisbeing.com/rv-arrival-and-set-up-checklist/

RV INSURANCE. (n.d.). Disadvantages of owning a Class A motorhome. Retrieved from https://rvinsurance.com/disadvantages-of-owning-a-class-A-motorhome/

RV LIFE. (n.d.). 5 great benefits of owning a Class C RV. Retrieved from https://rvlife.com/5-great-benefits-of-owning-a-class-c-rv/

RV LIFE. (n.d.). RV plumbing: Fixing RV water supply lines. Retrieved from https://rvlife.com/rv-plumbing-fixing-rv-water-supply-lines/

RV LIFE. (n.d.). How to prevent tire blowouts in RVs. Retrieved from https://rvlife.com/tire-blowouts-in-rvs/

RV LIFESTYLE. (n.d.). 10 reasons a Type B RV may be right for you. Retrieved from https://rvlifestyle.com/10-reasons-type-b-rv-may-right/

RV LIFESTYLE. (n.d.). The best camper vans: Class B motorhomes. Retrieved from https://rvlifestyle.com/best-camper-vans/

RV LIFESTYLE. (n.d.). Best rainy day camping activities for adults. Retrieved from https://rvlifestyle.com/best-rainy-day-camping-activities-for-adults/

RV LIFESTYLE. (n.d.). Clothes to pack for an RV trip. Retrieved from https://rvlifestyle.com/clothes-pack-rv-trip/

RV LIFESTYLE. (n.d.). RV breakdown checklist. Retrieved from https://rvlifestyle.com/rv-breakdown-checklist/

RV LIKE A PRO. (n.d.). How to take your RV out of winter storage. Retrieved from https://rvlikeapro.com/?p=809

RV OWNER HQ. (n.d.). Toy hauler cost. Retrieved from https://rvownerhq.com/toy-hauler-cost/

Bibliography

RV OWNER HQ. (n.d.). What does a Class B RV cost? Retrieved from https://rvownerhq.com/what-does-a-class-b-rv-cost/

RV SHARE. (n.d.). RV lifestyle: An in-depth guide. Retrieved from https://rvshare.com/blog/rv-lifestyle/

RV SHARE. (n.d.). How to set up at an RV campground for the first time. Retrieved from https://rvshare.com/blog/set-rv-campground-first-time/

RV TROOP. (n.d.). RV clothing. Retrieved from https://rvtroop.com/rv-clothing

SHELF COOKING. (n.d.). Make-ahead camping meals. Retrieved from https://shelfcooking.com/make-ahead-camping-meals/

SOWLERV. (n.d.). Top 20 RV camping quotes. Retrieved from https://sowlerv.com/top-20-rv-camping-quotes/

THE DYRT. (n.d.). RV clubs. Retrieved from https://thedyrt.com/magazine/lifestyle/rv-clubs/

THE OUTDOOR AUTHORITY. (n.d.). Things to do while camping. Retrieved from https://theoutdoorauthority.com/things-to-do-while-camping/

THE ROVING FOLEYS. (n.d.). The 6 essential accessories you will need in your RV kitchen. Retrieved from https://therovingfoleys.com/the-6-essential-accessories-you-will-need-in-your-rv-kitchen/

THE RV ATLAS. (n.d.). Pros and cons of the Class B RV. Retrieved from https://thervatlas.com/podcast/rvfta-130-pros-and-cons-of-the-class-b-rv/

TINY HOUSE DESIGN. (n.d.). RV toilet leaking: Common problems and how to fix them. Retrieved from https://tinyhousedesign.com/rv-toilet-leaking-common-problems-and-how-to-fix-them/

VERAVISE. (n.d.). Premade camping meals. Retrieved from https://veravise.com/premade-camping-meals/

VITTANA. (n.d.). 18 big pros and cons of owning a travel trailer. Retrieved from https://vittana.org/18-big-pros-and-cons-of-owning-a-travel-trailer

WERE THE RUSSOS. (n.d.). Must-have tools for your RV tool kit. Retrieved from https://weretherussos.com/must-have-tools-rv-tool-kit/

WERE THE RUSSOS. (n.d.). Pros and cons of RV dry camping (boondocking). Retrieved from https://weretherussos.com/pros-cons-rv-dry-camping-boondocking/

47 WEST TRAILERS. (n.d.). Toy hauler pros and cons. Retrieved from https://www.47westtrailers.com/blog/toy-hauler-pros-and-cons---36634

AMERICAN ADVENTURE INSURANCE. (n.d.). RV full-time living. Retrieved from https://www.aainsurance.com/blog/living-in-an-rv-full-time-everything-you-need-to-know/

BILL PLEMMONS RV. (n.d.). 5 amazing benefits of owning a Class A motorhome. Retrieved from https://www.billplemmonsrv.com/blog/5-amazing-benefits-of-owning-a-class-a-motorhome/

BLACK SERIES. (n.d.). What is a travel trailer? Retrieved from https://www.blackseries.net/blog/what-is-travel-trailer.html

CAMPANDA. (n.d.). Rainy day RV camping activities. Retrieved from https://www.campanda.com/magazine/rainy-day-rv-camping-activities/

COUNTRY LIVING. (n.d.). 30 camping quotes that'll make you want to pack up and go. Retrieved from https://www.countryliving.com/life/travel/g20916937/camping-quotes/

DAVE'S TRAVEL PAGES. (n.d.). 50 inspiring camping quotes: Best quotes about camping. Retrieved from https://www.davestravelpages.com/50-inspiring-camping-quotes-best-quotes-about-camping/

DO IT YOURSELF RV. (n.d.). Camping quotes. Retrieved from https://www.doityourselfrv.com/camping-quotes/

DO IT YOURSELF RV. (n.d.). 18 foods with a long shelf life for RV storage. Retrieved from https://www.doityourselfrv.com/foods-rv-storage/

DO IT YOURSELF RV. (n.d.). RV window leak. Retrieved from https://www.doityourselfrv.com/rv-window-leak/

FASTWAY TRAILER. (n.d.). Stay safe on the road by checking your breakaway cable. Retrieved from https://www.fastwaytrailer.com/blog/stay-safe-on-the-road-by-checking-your-breakaway-cable#:~:text=A%20breakaway%20cable%20is%20a,box%2C%20activating%20the%20trailer%20brakes

GENERAL RV. (n.d.). Class B motorhomes: A rising trend. Retrieved from https://www.generalrv.com/blog/class-b-motorhomes-rising-trend/

GENERAL RV. (n.d.). RVing 101: Misconceptions of owning an RV. Retrieved from https://www.generalrv.com/blog/rving-101-misconceptions-owning-rv/

GETAWAY COUPLE. (n.d.). Camper trailer. Retrieved from https://www.getawaycouple.com/camper-trailer/

GETAWAY COUPLE. (n.d.). Full-time RV living. Retrieved from https://www.getawaycouple.com/full-time-rv-living/

GETAWAY COUPLE. (n.d.). How much does an RV cost? You may be surprised. Retrieved from https://www.getawaycouple.com/how-much-does-an-rv-cost-you-may-be-suprised/

GETAWAY COUPLE. (n.d.). RV essentials. Retrieved from https://www.getawaycouple.com/rv-essentials/

GODOWNSIZE. (n.d.). Fifth wheel cost. Retrieved from https://www.godownsize.com/fifth-wheel-cost/

HUNKER. (n.d.). RV toilet not flushing. Retrieved from https://www.hunker.com/13400893/rv-toilet-not-flushing

JD POWER. (n.d.). What is a toy hauler? Retrieved from https://www.jdpower.com/rvs/shopping-guides/what-is-a-toy-hauler#:~:text=A%20toy%20hauler%20can%20cost,amenities%2C%20materials%2C%20and%20size

KETELSEN RV. (n.d.). Benefits of owning RV toy hauler. Retrieved from https://www.ketelsenrv.com/blog/benefits-of-owning-rv-toy-hauler/

KIDS FINANCIAL EDUCATION. (n.d.). 50 free outdoor activities for kids. Retrieved from https://www.kidsfinancialeducation.com/activities/free-outdoor-activities-kids/

LET'S TRAVEL FAMILY. (n.d.). RV kitchen accessories you must have. Retrieved from https://www.letstravelfamily.com/rv-kitchen-accessories-you-must-have/

LET'S TRAVEL FAMILY. (n.d.). RV must-haves you cannot live without. Retrieved from https://www.letstravelfamily.com/rv-must-haves-cannot-live-without/

MICHIGAN RV AND CAMPGROUNDS. (n.d.). RV toilet problems and what to do. Retrieved from https://www.michiganrvandcampgrounds.org/rv-toilet-problems-and-what-to-do/

MORTONS ON THE MOVE. (n.d.). Camping toiletries. Retrieved from https://www.mortonsonthemove.com/camping-toiletries/

MORTONS ON THE MOVE. (n.d.). Why does my RV battery keep dying? Retrieved from https://www.mortonsonthemove.com/rv-battery-keeps-dying/

Bibliography

MORTONS ON THE MOVE. (n.d.). RV tire blowout. Retrieved from https://www.mortonsonthemove.com/rv-tire-blowout/

MORTONS ON THE MOVE. (n.d.). RV tool kit. Retrieved from https://www.mortonsonthemove.com/rv-tool-kit/

MORTONS ON THE MOVE. (n.d.). What does RV stand for? Retrieved from https://www.mortonsonthemove.com/what-does-rv-stand-for/

MOTOR BISCUIT. (n.d.). The most common RV plumbing problems you know. Retrieved from https://www.motorbiscuit.com/most-common-rv-plumbing-problems-you-know/

MOTOR BISCUIT. (n.d.). What to do when you arrive at the campsite in your RV. Retrieved from https://www.motorbiscuit.com/what-do-when-arrive-campsite-rv/

OUTDOORSY. (n.d.). RV park discount clubs: Saving money. Retrieved from https://www.outdoorsy.com/blog/rv-park-discount-clubs-saving-money

OUTDOORSY. (n.d.). What is a toy hauler and who rents them? Retrieved from https://www.outdoorsy.com/blog/what-is-a-toy-hauler-and-who-rents-them?wb-auto_radius=true&wb-currency=USD&wb-filter%5Bkeywords%5D=toy%20hauler&wb-instant_book=true&wb-locale=en-us&wb-page%5Blimit%5D=4&wb-page%5Boffset%5D=0

OUTDOORSY. (n.d.). What is an RV? Retrieved from https://www.outdoorsy.com/blog/what-is-an-rv?wb-auto_radius=true&wb-currency=USD&wb-instant_book=true&wb-locale=en-us&wb-page%5Blimit%5D=4&wb-page%5Boffset%5D=0

OUTDOORSY. (n.d.). Why it's called a fifth wheel RV. Retrieved from https://www.outdoorsy.com/blog/why-its-called-a-fifth-wheel-rv

PPL MOTORHOMES. (n.d.). About Class C motorhomes. Retrieved from https://www.pplmotorhomes.com/about-class-c-motorhomes#:~:text=Class%20C%20motorhomes%2C%20sometimes%20called,with%20an%20attached%20cab%20section

PROGRESSIVE. (n.d.). Pros and cons of a pop-up camper. Retrieved from https://www.progressive.com/lifelanes/adventure/pros-and-cons-of-a-pop-up-camper/

RV.COM. (n.d.). The basics to RV roof leak repair. Retrieved from https://www.rv.com/servicing-care/safety-maintenance/the-basics-to-rv-roof-leak-repair/

RVEZY. (n.d.). How to winterize an RV. Retrieved from https://www.rvezy.com/blog/how-to-winterize-rv

RVING KNOW HOW. (n.d.). Class A motorhome cost. Retrieved from https://www.rvingknowhow.com/class-a-motorhome-cost/

RVING PLANET. (n.d.). 10 can't-miss tips for storing your new RV. Retrieved from https://www.rvingplanet.com/blog/10-cant-miss-tips-for-storing-your-new-rv/

RVNGO. (n.d.). 10 rainy day activities for campers. Retrieved from https://www.rvngo.com/onthego/outdoor-enjoyment/10-rainy-day-activities-for-campers/

RV TRAVEL. (n.d.). Where to you hitch your breakaway cable? Retrieved from https://www.rvtravel.com/where-to-you-hitch-your-breakaway-cable/

SMITHSONIAN MAGAZINE. (n.d.). A brief history of the RV. Retrieved from https://www.smithsonianmag.com/innovation/brief-history-rv-180970195/

STOR-IT. (n.d.). RV storage: 12 tips for properly storing your RV. Retrieved from https://www.stor-it.com/blog/rv-storage-12-tips-for-properly-storing-your-rv/

THE RV GEEKS. (n.d.). Why does my RV battery keep dying? Retrieved from https://www.thervgeeks.com/why-does-my-rv-battery-keep-dying/

THE RV GEEKS. (n.d.). Winter RV living. Retrieved from https://www.thervgeeks.com/winter-rv-living/

THE WAYWARD HOME. (n.d.). 40 important tools you must have in your RV tool kit. Retrieved from https://www.thewaywardhome.com/40-important-tools-you-must-have-in-your-rv-tool-kit/

TRANSWEST. (n.d.). Pros and cons of 5th wheel campers. Retrieved from https://www.transwest.com/rv/blog/pros-and-cons-of-5th-wheel-campers/

ULTRAHEAT. (n.d.). How to deal with a leaking window on your RV. Retrieved from https://www.ultraheat.com/post/how-to-deal-with-a-leaking-window-on-your-rv

WASHINGTON POST. (n.d.). A million Americans live in RVs. Retrieved from https://www.washingtonpost.com/business/2018/11/12/million-americans-live-rvs-meet-modern-nomads/

WISEBREAD. (n.d.). 50 ways to have free outdoor fun. Retrieved from https://www.wisebread.com/50-ways-to-have-free-outdoor-fun

ABOUT THE AUTHOR

Rain Tucker's journey into the world of RV camping was shaped by the profound influence of her grandparents during her formative years. From childhood, she embraced the RV lifestyle and eagerly purchased her first RV as a young adult, marking the beginning of her adventurous solo RVing days. Now, as a parent with a partner, two children, and a furry companion, Rain's family continues to embark on extended RV trips for months at a time. With a lifetime of experience navigating the intricacies of life on the road, Rain and her family possess an intimate understanding of the nuances of RV living.

Printed in Great Britain
by Amazon